T0372437

lazy
love

lazy
love

RECOGNIZING AND REVERSING
——————— THE 4 THREATS ———————
TO ANY SUCCESSFUL RELATIONSHIP

KEION
HENDERSON

Faith
Words

New York • Nashville

Copyright © 2024 by Keion D. Henderson

Cover design by Kristen Paige Andrews
Cover photograph by Micah Kandros
Cover copyright © 2024 by Hachette Book Group, Inc.

Hachette Book Group supports the right to free expression and the value of copyright. The purpose of copyright is to encourage writers and artists to produce the creative works that enrich our culture.

The scanning, uploading, and distribution of this book without permission is a theft of the author's intellectual property. If you would like permission to use material from the book (other than for review purposes), please contact permissions@hbgusa.com. Thank you for your support of the author's rights.

FaithWords
Hachette Book Group
1290 Avenue of the Americas, New York, NY 10104
faithwords.com
twitter.com/faithwords

First Edition: August 2024

FaithWords is a division of Hachette Book Group, Inc. The FaithWords name and logo are registered trademarks of Hachette Book Group, Inc.

The publisher is not responsible for websites (or their content) that are not owned by the publisher.

The Hachette Speakers Bureau provides a wide range of authors for speaking events. To find out more, go to hachettespeakersbureau.com or email HachetteSpeakers@hbgusa.com.

FaithWords books may be purchased in bulk for business, educational, or promotional use. For information, please contact your local bookseller or the Hachette Book Group Special Markets Department at special.markets@hbgusa.com.

Unless otherwise indicated, Scriptures are taken from the Holy Bible, New International Version®, NIV®. Copyright © 1973, 1978, 1984, 2011 by Biblica, Inc.™ Used by permission of Zondervan. All rights reserved worldwide. www.zondervan.com The "NIV" and "New International Version" are trademarks registered in the United States Patent and Trademark Office by Biblica, Inc.™

Scriptures noted ASV are from the American Standard Version. Public domain.

Scriptures noted ESV are taken from the ESV® Bible (The Holy Bible, English Standard Version®), © 2001 by Crossway, a publishing ministry of Good News Publishers. Used by permission. All rights reserved. The ESV text may not be quoted in any publication made available to the public by a Creative Commons license. The ESV may not be translated in whole or in part into any other language.

Scriptures noted KJV are taken from the King James Version. Public domain.

Scriptures noted MSG are taken from The Message, copyright © 1993, 2002, 2018 by Eugene H. Peterson. Used by permission of NavPress. All rights reserved. Represented by Tyndale House Publishers.

Scriptures noted NKJV are taken from the New King James Version®. Copyright © 1982 by Thomas Nelson. Used by permission. All rights reserved.

Scriptures noted NLT are taken from the Holy Bible, New Living Translation, copyright ©1996, 2004, 2015 by Tyndale House Foundation. Used by permission of Tyndale House Publishers, Carol Stream, Illinois 60188. All rights reserved.

Library of Congress Cataloging-in-Publication Data

Names: Henderson, Keion, author.
Title: Lazy love : recognizing and reversing the 4 threats to any successful relationship / Keion Henderson.
Description: First edition. | New York : Faith Words, 2024. |
Identifiers: LCCN 2024001370 | ISBN 9781546006831 (hardcover) | ISBN 9781546006855 (ebook)
Subjects: LCSH: Love—Religious aspects—Christianity. | Interpersonal relations—Religious aspects—Christianity.
Classification: LCC BV4639 .H355 2024 | DDC 241/.6777—dc23/eng/20240222
LC record available at https://lccn.loc.gov/2024001370

ISBNs: 978-1-5460-0683-1 (hardcover); 978-1-5460-0685-5 (ebook)

Printed in the United States of America

LSC-C

Printing 1, 2024

My dear wife,

Thank you for helping me to actually realize and know the true meaning of love. It's not the vows that keep us together, it's the love we have for each other. Prior to you, I was unworthy to tell this story. Because of you I am now worthy! I owe you my all.

Contents

——— 5 ———

THREAT #4: CONFUSING SEX WITH INTIMACY DUE TO LACK OF EROS

1

Refusing to Settle for Lazy Love

*Everyone who loves has been born of God
and knows God. Whoever does not love
does not know God, because God is love.*

1 JOHN 4:7-8

*You can give without loving, but you
can never love without giving.*

ROBERT LOUIS STEVENSON

CHAPTER 1

Love, Actually

Loving others always costs us something and requires effort.
And you have to decide to do it on purpose. You can't wait
for a feeling to motivate you.

—Joyce Meyer

I suddenly felt more alone than I ever had.

Catching a glimpse of my reflection in the restaurant's glass storefront, I hardly recognized myself. There I sat, all alone at a small café table, hunched over a bowl of potato soup. Around me the hum of animated voices underscored my solitary silence. While the smell of my meager meal reminded me why it was one of my favorites, I could barely taste its flavor. How in the world had I gotten to this place?

There's nothing wrong with eating alone or enjoying the pleasant solitude of your own company. But this was not my experience in that moment. Being surrounded by other diners in a busy restaurant simply aimed a spotlight on my current status as a recently divorced, single man. Sitting there and finishing my soup—because

I refused to give in to my discomfort—I reflected on how and why I found myself alone at this point in my life.

I had never expected to be single again, and I went through the checklist most men might consider after a recent breakup, the catalog of reasons that made sense and explained this singular status. While I was far from perfect, I was never abusive. I went through other plausible reasons for the failure of our relationship but found none that applied. Despite the fact that I had initiated our divorce, not my ex-wife, I struggled to explain how and exactly when our relationship had shifted.

How did I get to a place where I could not forgive, where I could not communicate what I was feeling? When did our mutual respect deteriorate into ambivalence? Why did our jointly held relational security suddenly disappear, only to be replaced by individual insecurities?

As I pondered the contributing factors leading to our divorce and my current singleness, I realized those four factors—forgiveness, communication, respect, and security—were essential elements, but not the ultimate cause of our breakup. In that moment I realized I was alone again not for lack of any of these four.

I was alone again because of lazy love.

IT'S COMPLICATED

Simply put, my capacity to love had gradually atrophied. The end of my marriage occurred because slowly and almost imperceptibly I had defaulted to lazy love, relying on my own abilities and tendencies rather than drawing on the Greater Love beyond myself. After that moment of epiphany about why I was suddenly alone again, I began studying the problem of lazy love, its causes and, greater still, its remedies.

During the course of this exploration, I asked and overheard how people—family and friends, church members and visitors, Christians and non-Christians, marrieds and singles, strangers and acquaintances, women and men—described their love life or relationship status. The most common response and refrain on love that I heard? "It's complicated."

While I understand that sharing whom we love and how we love is rarely simple and straightforward, I also wonder when relationships became so complicated. Or perhaps love has always been messy and chaotic, irrational and disruptive, and people are finally willing to admit it. But I suspect the problem stems from settling for much less than we were made to enjoy with one another.

When I press in on what people mean when they say "complicated," I often end up agreeing with their assessment. Co-parents but not partners. Friends with benefits but no commitment. Exes who try to move on but can't let go. Seekers always looking ahead for what they don't have and who they can't find. Spouses estranged to the point of being strangers. The twists and turns, the layers and longings—yes, "complicated" sums it up. Complicated because the loving connections we long to experience always seem elusive.

I recently thought about the state of modern love on the day most associated with it—Valentine's Day. Whether you enjoy February 14 by celebrating love or actively resist the cultural and media hoopla around it, there's no denying that Valentine's Day continues to be big business. According to *Forbes*, US consumer spending on that holiday in 2023 was up about 8 percent from the previous year, setting a record of approximately $26 *billion*.[1] That's a lot of chocolate, roses, and romantic dinners!

But Valentine's Day is not just about romantic love anymore. Beyond the flowers, cards, and candy for sweethearts, people also use the day to celebrate appreciation for various other loved ones and relationships—family members, close friends, neighbors and community members, first responders, and even pets. Female friends often gather to celebrate "Galentine's Day," a nod to their enduring friendship rather than the complications of romance. These extensions seem only fitting because the origin of St. Valentine's Day had little to nothing to do with romance. According to historians, "Valentine's Day, in fact, originated as a liturgical feast to celebrate the decapitation of a third-century Christian martyr, or perhaps two."[2]

But perfect love isn't celebrated just in February. On any given day, a quick scan of what's trending on Facebook, Instagram, and TikTok provides a snapshot: #foreverlove, #youmyboo, #loveher, #hesthe1, #couples, #taken, #happilyeverafter. These barely scratch the surface of the way love is portrayed, presented, and promoted in everything from Disney movies and romance novels to reality dating shows and even church singles events. Yes, Christians are just as guilty as anyone else when it comes to idealizing marriage and romantic love.

Which brings us back to that love refrain you've likely heard or even said yourself: "It's complicated."

LOVE DEFINED

To get a clearer, uncomplicated understanding of love, the history of Valentine's Day isn't much help. So I turned to the greatest source of wisdom I know, the Bible. Love in all its forms is mentioned in Scripture around 361 times by my count. With so much to say about love, surely God's Word must contain a basic definition that can be applied to the various kinds of human relationships, not just that of husband and wife.

When it comes to Scriptures about love, many people immediately turn to 1 Corinthians 13. You know, "Love is patient. Love is kind. It does not envy or boast," and so on—familiar words often found on wall plaques, greeting cards, and framed embroidery given as wedding presents. As a pastor asked to officiate at weddings, I'm frequently instructed to include this familiar biblical passage on love. While I'm happy to include the couple's choice of Scripture, I also like to point out what I believe is a more foundational passage defining love, one that goes beyond just describing it, one that lays a foundation for any and all human interactions and relationships:

> God is love. Whoever lives in love lives in God, and God in them…We love because he first loved us. Whoever claims to love God yet hates a brother or sister is a liar. For whoever does not love their brother and sister, whom they have seen, cannot love God, whom they have not seen. And he has given us this command: Anyone who loves God must also love their brother and sister. (1 John 4:16, 19–21)

How do we begin to define love? Notice the two elements revealed here. First, God *is* love. So when you're talking about love, you're actually talking about God. The two are synonymous—God and love. Apparently, love is the essence of who God is and what He's all about.

Second, because God is love, we are conduits of His love. John points out in this passage that we love because God first loved us. This makes sense because we know our Creator made us in His own image. As the source of love, God designed us to reflect His loving nature but also to channel and focus it based on our experience of His love. Therefore, it's impossible to love someone else if you don't love God. And don't miss the brilliant, practical logic John uses here: How can you love God—whom you've never seen—when you can't love the other people all around you?

Reinforcing this truth, Jesus told His followers, "By this everyone will know that you are my disciples, if you love one another" (John 13:35). I don't believe He meant that we should always display affection or bring the warm fuzzies wherever we go. But I do believe Jesus intends for us to understand that loving others is an active process. Love requires action: "But be doers of the word, and not hearers only" (James 1:22 NKJV).

Which brings me to the passage from God's Word that inspired me to write this book and that makes our call to love loud and clear:

> God is not unjust; he will not forget your work and the love you have shown him as you have helped his people and continue to help them. We want each of you to show this same diligence to the very end, so that what you hope for may be fully realized. We do not want you to become lazy, but to imitate those who through faith and patience inherit what has been promised. (Hebrews 6:10–12)

What's the opposite of diligent faith here? What naturally happens when we fail to love diligently? We grow lazy. Our capacity to love gets lazy.

Instead of "lazy," other translations use "sluggish" (ESV), "dull and indifferent" (NLT), and "slothful" (KJV). The Greek word used in the original text is *nothros*. Used literally, *nothros* might describe the tarnish that forms on unpolished silver over time or the way a well-used candle no longer burns brightly. Applied more descriptively, especially regarding how we live by faith and walk in love, *nothros* implies apathy, indifference, being lukewarm.

Without prevention and provocation, most of us grow lazy over time.

We settle for relationships that don't satisfy.

We feel entitled to withhold ourselves from those we want to love.

We fear risking our hearts because they will get broken.

We misunderstand the implications of showing true affection.

We confuse sexual encounters with divine intimacy.

We settle for lazy love without realizing it.

LESSONS IN LOVE

From the moment human beings arrive in this world, we are shaped, scarred, slapped, and soothed by the power of human love, with each experience contributing different associations and expectations regarding how we give and receive love. And no matter how loving, caring, and emotionally healthy our household may have been when we were growing up, human beings carry the indelible scar of selfishness (what theologians might define as original sin) within us at birth.

Babies learn how to love from their parents, who have their own wounds and deficits when it comes to giving and receiving love. In other words, no matter how well our parents may have loved us, they still loved us imperfectly because of their own inheritance of imperfect love from their parents. We will explore more about how human beings learn to love and be loved in chapters 2 and 3.

As we mature and grow, our individual experiences also shape how we define love, receive love, and learn to love others. It doesn't take very many class parties, school dances, social media posts, or unreciprocated valentines before our fear of rejection and abandonment kicks in. Our sexuality is also intertwined into the midst of this ever-changing formula, fueling lust with seemingly out-of-control hormones or channeling our passions and desires into physical expressions.

Since God made us as sexual beings and since He created us in His own image, we know that our sexuality is a divine gift. Like so many other aspects of our humanity, though, sex has an incredible capacity to either draw us closer to God and other people in healthy ways or pull us away toward destructive tendencies. Our sexuality tends to reflect our brokenness, and our brokenness tends to reveal itself in our sexuality.

Consequently, as we become adults and begin practicing what we've learned about love, we usually discover how to get at least a little bit of the affection and attention we crave in other, not so healthy ways. Whether that's through flirting, seducing, manipulating, and using others or turning to what we can watch on our phones and flat screens, these lessons in settling-for-less tend to damage our understanding of and capacity for love as well. We long to be seen and known and loved and to see and know and love others, but the process gets challenging...and complicated.

Over time and through experience, many people grow protective and defensive, guarding their hearts from what they assume will be eventual inevitable pain and suffering. They begin to doubt the kind of love celebrated on Valentine's Day actually exists, considering it instead as a kind of mirage, an unattainable oasis always taunting them. They may grow cynical and doubt that such ideal love can ever exist. And maybe it can't, at least not in the way our culture brands love, but that awareness doesn't eliminate the longing deep in their soul to be known, accepted, and loved unconditionally.

Lazy love can be overcome—not just in our romantic relationships, but in all relationships. With ourselves and with God. With other people. Family and friends. Coworkers and colleagues. Those who agree with us and those who radically disagree with what we believe. Lazy love prevents us from experiencing the deep, soulful fulfillment we long to know. It keeps us from being known and enjoyed by those around us. And it stops us from stepping out to give all we are without expecting anything in return.

But lazy love can be overcome.

When you identify the threats undermining your relationships, you can then correct and align your relational longings with your choices, motivations, and actions.

And that's what this book is all about.

LAST BUT NOT LEAST

Why do you suppose the writer of Hebrews doesn't want to see the recipients of his epistle grow lazy? And by application, why would God not want us to grow lazy? Isn't lazy love better than no love at all?

The answer to this question emerges when we compare laziness to some of the other sins mentioned in the Bible, particularly those known as the seven deadly sins. These sins, also known as the cardinal vices, are not mentioned anywhere in Scripture in a group, but they have a long tradition in the history of the Christian faith. For our purposes, they illustrate what's remarkably distinct about lazy love when held up against other sins. And whether you've heard of them grouped together as the seven deadlies before, I suspect you've struggled with each of them at some point in your life:

First, there's pride.

Second, greed.

Third, wrath.

Fourth, envy.

Fifth, lust.

Sixth, gluttony.

And last but not least, sloth.

Notice anything different about that last deadly sin? Did sloth stand out to you when compared to the others listed for any reason? Here's what I see: The first six deadly sins are the result of too much of something.

Pride is when you have too much love and appreciation for yourself and your own interests. Greed is when you have too much desire for something else, money or love or achievements or whatever you think will satisfy your inner hunger. Wrath is when you have too much anger. It's okay to be angry, but when you allow it to poison your attitude or motivate destructive actions, then of course it becomes sinful.

Lust is too much emotional, physical, and sensual pleasure. You objectify others and view your fulfillment as transactional gratification. Gluttony is too much appetite, usually for food, although it could be for fame or prescription meds or really anything to which you're addicted. The focus is on getting as much as you can in order to fill an insatiable appetite of some kind.

Yes, all of these first six major sin categories are the result of too much, a hoarder's attitude toward whatever aspect of desire you're seeking to satisfy. If a little of something is good, then a lot must be better. Only it's the excess that leads to addiction—enough is never enough.

The last one, though, which is traditionally known as sloth more than laziness, is the result of *not enough* of something. Instead of an excess, sloth results from a lack of energy, initiative, and momentum. Sloth lets things slide and resists responsibility. It looks the other way instead of turning the other cheek. It crosses the street to avoid having to help someone in need. It takes the easy way out every time. Sloth revels in lazy love.

But the two—slothful and lazy—are not exactly the same despite often being used synonymously. There's a subtle difference that leads to a huge understanding of what's at stake.

LAZY DAZE

Ever have one of those lazy days where you just lie around and think about what you should do but don't feel like doing? There's a reason for that. What we often call laziness is frequently the result of exhaustion, fatigue, and lack of energy. This kind of laziness is when you don't have the energy to do what you have the responsibility to do even though you're willing and want to do it. This form of inaction is often a signal from your mind, body, and soul that you've been running on empty for too long. You need rest.

As we know from Genesis, even the Lord Himself rested on the seventh day after creating everything over the previous six days. Because He's God, I suspect that He didn't need the rest to recharge the way we do. But because He knew His creation needed cycles and seasons of rest, He set a clear example.

So when you're dragging yourself out of bed in the morning or trying to do what has to be done even though you don't feel like doing it, this kind of laziness has a cause and a remedy. When you're deprived of sleep and don't have the rest you need, you will naturally struggle to muster enough energy to do the things you want to do. You might say, "I don't feel like doing the laundry today. I don't feel like doing my Bible study. I don't feel like praying. I don't feel like going to work. I don't feel like running your bathwater. I don't feel like putting mayonnaise on your sandwich—it might be dry, but you won't go hungry!"

When you're depleted and in need of sabbath rest, God does not consider your inaction sinful in and of itself. If you use your exhaustion as an excuse or as a way to manipulate others, then obviously you're getting into trouble. But simply not feeling like doing something because you lack what you need—that kind of laziness is not the kind included in the seven deadly sins. It's not the kind referenced by the author of Hebrews when he wrote, "We do not want you to become lazy" (6:12).

While the word used here can be translated as "slothful" (KJV) or "lazy" (NIV), another connotation from the original Greek means "no thrust." There's no initiative, momentum, or drive—not because you're tired or lacking fuel—*but because you willfully choose not to engage*. This refers not simply to lack of energy and incapacity for initiative, which I'm calling lazy. No, this kind of slothfulness has the capacity to act but deliberately withholds.

The sin of sloth is disinterest, disengagement, distraction, and destruction by choosing not to give, act, love, or risk.

Slothfulness like this is about self-defense, protecting yourself, and attaining what's in it for you. For example, you might act interested in your partner's description of her day, but you're tuned out and waiting until you can rant about your own. You might say you don't care where you go to eat, but you really don't want to be responsible for his expectations of the evening. Rather than break up with someone or have that honest conversation that terrifies you, you passively keep things status quo even though your heart is no longer engaged in the relationship.

This slothful brand of lazy love is tepid, fickle, wishy-washy, and lukewarm. It's all the things that real love is not. God's Word tells us the Lord would prefer that we be hot or cold rather than in between. There is no middle ground with Him, and therefore there is no middle ground when it comes to love.

The author of Hebrews makes God's position on this clear, indicating that He wants us to quit being slothful. To quit acting like someone who has lost their enthusiasm and excitement because their circumstances aren't going the way they wanted and expected. To stop pretending to have an authentic faith while just going through the motions to save face with regard to what others think.

Be hot or cold, but don't be lukewarm. If you're going to do this thing called love, whether it be for God or your significant other or your children, then you've got to do it with everything you have. Because slothfulness has nothing to do with energy. It has to do with the condition of your heart and your attitude toward God and others.

Lazy love keeps you stuck in place. You say the same things over and over again. You have the same arguments again and again, following the same old scripts. You don't listen and you don't care if you're heard. You want to break free but are afraid to try—or you just don't care. You may have grown cynical because of past disappointments and devastations. You may have secretly vowed that no one would ever hurt you again the way you were once hurt.

Even though you're not going anywhere with lazy love, it still requires so much energy. Because deep down, you know you're not experiencing the love you were made to receive and to give. Defending yourself and settling for less-than-best drains you and results in little or no return. Lazy love will never become crazy love unless you risk wanting more and trusting God to meet your needs.

FULL-CIRCLE LOVE

In order to combat your tendency toward lazy love, you don't need to try harder—you simply must expand your awareness of what it means to love and to trust God in all areas of your life. This is why it's important to identify the threats encroaching on your relationships that matter most to you. As you grow closer to God, you also grow in your understanding and capacity for love. With God as your foundation for love, you discover that all facets of how you relate and love extend from the way He first loved you. You don't have to rely on your own capacity to love because you have access to a much greater, limitless, unconditional source of love.

In fact, this divine foundational love—the Greek word used in the New Testament is *agape*—is essential to the good news of the gospel and the goodness of God's grace. According to God's Word, three other kinds of love grow out of agape: *phileo*, the love of friendship; *storge*, the love within families and dutiful relationships; and *eros*, the sensual and romantic love between a husband and wife. While all four types coexist and often overlap, I'm convinced exploring them in this progression—agape, phileo, storge, and eros—reveals a full-circle pattern that reinforces those two foundational aspects of love from 1 John 4 that I mentioned previously: God is love, and His love defines us.

Understanding these four types of love clearly and personally provides a clarifying contrast to what you've been settling for— neighbors you see but don't know, coworkers you're forced to trust despite misgivings, "frenemies" who perpetuate passive-aggressive encounters, partners whom you're afraid to hold accountable, lovers with whom you are not intimate.

As we consider each of these four types of love, and the major threat that undermines them, I hope you will be inspired and challenged to reflect on how you love, why you love, and what stands in the way of loving. This is the path forward through lazy love, leading to an awareness of your areas of wounding and how they influence your capacity to love as revealed in these four relational areas. With a keener understanding of your wounds, you can then experience greater healing and become more intentional in how you give and receive love.

We will begin with agape, the unconditional and supernatural love God has for us as His children, because it is paramount. You may have heard of this kind of love before and how it expresses the unfathomable, limitless, merciful, and eternal love our heavenly Father has for us. God's willingness to send His only Son, Jesus, to live as a human being here on earth and then die an excruciating death on the cross in order to pay for our sins—that's the essence of agape. It's summed up by John 3:16: "This is how much God loved the world: He gave his Son, his one and only Son. And this is why: so that no one need be destroyed; by believing in him, anyone can have a whole and lasting life" (MSG).

Phileo expresses the kind of loving bond formed in healthy, lasting friendships. It's the broadest kind of love described in Scripture and reflects how followers of Jesus relate to one another: "By this everyone will know that you are my disciples, if you love one another" (John 13:35). Phileo love is about connection, community, compassion, and caring among people who have experienced the divine love of their heavenly Father.

Storge may be the least familiar kind of love mentioned in the Bible. It describes the kind of love parents naturally have for their children and children for their mother and father. This type of love emerges in the way that God often related to the people of Israel. Rather than respond to the Lord as their loving Father, however, the Israelites often rebelled and turned away from Him. Their stubborn hard-heartedness became a major obstacle in their ability to love. Forgiveness removes that obstacle and reflects an integral ingredient, not just in storge love but in all types. God promises us, "I will give you a new heart and put a new spirit in you; I will remove from you your heart of stone and give you a heart of flesh" (Ezek. 36:26).

Finally, eros is likely the kind of love that reveals your greatest challenges with giving and receiving love. Eros was the Greek god of love and sexual desire, and the name is the origin of our word "erotic." In the Bible, "eros" is applied to the union of husband and wife, becoming one flesh through their love in body and spirit. Struggles with sexual brokenness were just as common in ancient times as now, but God's Word reserves eros for marriage—which is also used as a picture of Christ's relationship to His bride, the church. In our world today, eros has been prioritized over the other types of love and corrupted in its biblical usage.

By returning to agape, however, and building from your relationship with God, you can experience a revival of love in all areas of your life.

TIMELESS AND TIMELY

If you want to expand your capacity to love and overcome lazy love once and for all, then you must begin by focusing on your relationship with God. You might say you love Him, but what does that mean to you? How do you show Him? How much time do you spend with Him?

Jesus provided answers to these questions after He was asked by one of the Jewish teachers of the Law, "Of all the commandments, which is the most important?" And Jesus told him, "Love the Lord your God with all your heart and with all your soul and with all your mind and with all your strength" (Mark 12:30).

Christ's answer remains timeless and timely for us today. God wants us to love Him with all we are and all we have—heart, soul, mind, and body. It's no secret that He's a jealous God and doesn't want us worshipping idols or loving anything or anyone more than Him. In fact, Jesus is referencing a commandment (remember the teacher's question) recorded in Deuteronomy 6:4–5.

Loving God with all you've got leaves no room for lazy love to creep in. Because lazy love thrives when you focus on yourself—not on God and not on others. Returning to the answer Jesus gave that teacher, it's no coincidence that He said the second-greatest commandment was to "love your neighbor as yourself" (Mark 12:31). We love God, and because we love Him, we're able to love others.

You picked up this book for a reason, my friend.

You're not lazy if you want to know how to be more loving.

Overcoming lazy love begins by no longer refusing to settle for less than God's best!

CHAPTER 2

We Are All Made to Love

Love makes your soul crawl out from its hiding place.
—Zora Neale Hurston

Alexander the Great and John Legend may not seem to have much in common. If you know me and my personal interests, though—particularly my love of ancient history and contemporary music—you won't be surprised by my fascination with each of them. I suspect you might discover, just as I have, two intriguing approaches to love inspired by them. Because when it comes to gaining insight about lazy love and how to overcome it, we can focus on either power or perseverance. Please allow me to explain.

Following in the footsteps of his father, King Philip II of Macedonia, Alexander seems to have thrived on conquest. Even as a boy of twelve, Alexander showed courageous determination to achieve his goals by taming and training an enormous, fierce stallion named Bucephalus, which became his trusted steed for battle over most of Alexander's life. After taming this wild animal, Alexander conquered education, and he was tutored at age thirteen by none other than Aristotle. By the time he was sixteen, his father trusted

Alexander so much that he left him in charge of Macedonia while Philip went off to battle. Alexander not only maintained the kingdom but organized and led a cavalry to defeat a renowned group of local mercenaries known as the Sacred Band of Thebes at the Battle of Chaeronea.[1]

Alexander went on to become one of the greatest leaders and military strategists of all time. In battle after battle, he found a way to outmaneuver his adversaries, usually by applying his greatest strengths to their greatest vulnerabilities. When his father, Philip II, was assassinated, Alexander, at twenty years old, became king of Macedonia. From this base he went on to conquer Sardes, Tyre, Egypt (where the city of Alexandria, named for him, endures today), Persia, and India. He never rested on his triumphs for long because he apparently kept his sights set on the next battle, the next conquest, the next enemy to defeat, and the next prize to add to his empire.[2]

Sounds a lot like the relationship pattern of many people I've known!

MADE TO LOVE

A radically different approach than what we find with Alexandrian conquests comes from one of my favorite songs, "Made to Love," performed by John Legend. This is one of those songs that I wake up humming some mornings or that pop into my head at various times. I always welcome this particular song because of its simple but profound lyrical message. When reinforced by John's rich, silky baritone, the words of this love song echo with what I consider to be the essence of who Jesus is; as God's Son, Jesus was indeed sent here for you—and for me. And the refrain reminds us that we are made to love, which expresses our divine purpose succinctly and directly.

While I appreciate and admire the artistry of its lyrics, and I adore how John performs it, this song resonates as an anthem of agape love for me. Jesus said, "I have come that they may have life, and have it to the full" (John 10:10)—or, if I may paraphrase: "I was sent here for you. I came because I love you and want you to know what love really is."

By coming here for us, knowing He would be mocked and ridiculed by many, arrested and crucified by others, Jesus proved His love. He says He will come again (see John 14:3) and, as Paul reminds us in Romans, demonstrates that nothing can separate us from the love of His Father—now our Father, too (see Rom. 8:38–39). Even when we reject God and rebel against Him, He is always there for us. Jesus is willing to come back no matter how resistant we are to His love. He perseveres as He stands at the door of our hearts and knocks (see Rev. 3:20), just as the Father perseveres by running toward us when our prodigal hearts return home to Him.

Because God is love, we are made to love—and empowered to love others beyond our human capacity. Left to our own resources and limitations, we inevitably love ourselves more than we are capable of loving our neighbors. We don't like to suffer with others in their pain or work through the conflicts that require time, patience, and grace. Rather than dig into someone else's trauma, how they learned or didn't learn to love, not to mention our own trauma, we quit and settle for so much less. Giving up is the ultimate definition of lazy love.

Giving up closes the door on becoming all that God made you to be.

Because we are all made to love.

SUSTAINED SURVIVAL

Have you ever stopped to consider why you love the way you love?

Loving is hardwired into you—body, mind, and soul—as much as breathing, eating, drinking, sleeping, and survival. From the moment you were born, something in you has needed to, wanted to, and longed to connect with other people. First, you were forced to rely on your parents or caregivers, who taught you so much about how to love, both intentionally and implicitly. Your siblings, grandparents, extended family, and close friends continued to activate the parts of you that come together when you love.

At birth, you learned to love as a matter of survival and reliance. Simply put, you—along with every human being—were helpless when born into this world. Infants cannot focus their eyes, coordinate their movements, move their bodies any distance, or sit up, let alone stand. They need direct assistance to be fed, burped, comforted to sleep, and cleaned and changed. They are totally dependent on those responsible for their care.

Even once a baby grows into a toddler and proceeds through development to adolescence and young adulthood, they rely on the people around them to continue meeting their needs, if not physically then emotionally, psychologically, and relationally. Children learn socialization by playing with peers and interacting with others at their developmental level. In addition to immediate and extended family members, everyone grows with the assistance of teachers, coaches, mentors, neighbors, pastors, and medical professionals. At a basic level, the goal is for independence and interdependence to be balanced in the healthy tension required for humans to individuate and be self-sufficient as well as to relate and be socially connected in healthy ways.

If you received all you needed from those around you when you were growing up, then you may not suffer from lazy love as much as those who struggled and lacked what they needed. We will explore more about the impact our needs have in chapter 3, which is focused on how we are all made to receive love. But assuming most of your basic needs were met consistently during your growth into adulthood, then you would have not only received what you needed but absorbed what those around you modeled. Even if you didn't have all your needs met and continue to overcome setbacks, you still are made to love.

Because love is not simply a matter of survival.

Love is how God—the essence of love who first loved us—designed us.

LEARNING TO LOVE

While it's easy to say that loving is initially a matter of survival—being kindly disposed toward those responsible for your survival and well-being—it's more than that. Your ability to love grows along with the rest of you across your lifetime unless, of course, certain factors delay, hinder, or impede your development. As you grow, your capacity to love extends beyond physical touch to include emotions, thoughts, and actions expressed in a spectrum of loving ways depending on the contextual nature of your relationships.

Obviously, you learned to love your parents and siblings distinct from the way you learned to love your friends and the peer groups to which you belonged. As your body matured going into your teen years, your attractions toward members of the opposite sex developed and matured as well, which led to new aspects—and all those complications—of loving. Maturing into adulthood, you discovered new forms of love—love for your purpose, for your team, for your ideals, for your leaders. Throughout all these forms of love, new facets emerged in a myriad of ways. We need not debate whether love is an emotion, an experience, a physical sensation, a choice, an action, or a sacrifice—it is all these and more.

Experiences of love vary as much as the individuals caught up in them. But when a human being loves another, regardless of the context and the kind of love expressed, what actually goes into that moment? Why do we love the way we do? Why do some people seem to love more naturally and instinctively than others?

Like most human capacities, love includes the converging of a variety of factors—physical, neurological, emotional, social, and cultural. Seen through these lenses, each of the four biblical types of love we're exploring reveals an aspect of how God made us to love in various, complex ways. You were created to love in ways that are physical, sensual, and sexual, which the Bible calls eros love. You were created to love in ways that are emotional, psychological, and cooperative, hallmarks of phileo love. You were created to love in ways that are loyal, enduring, and selfless, qualities of storge love. And the basis for all of these ways to love is the way God designed you to love Him and to love others with His love—the kind of love called agape.

Let's explore each of these briefly and consider their relevance for how you are made to love.

BIOLOGY 101

Physically and biologically, God designed us to reflect His image in two primary, distinct ways: "So God created mankind in his own image, in the image of God he created them; male and female he created them" (Gen. 1:27). In addition to creating humans in His own image, "God blessed them and said to them, 'Be fruitful and increase in number; fill the earth and subdue it'" (Gen. 1:28).

These two facts—that we're created as male and female in God's own image and instructed by our Creator to procreate—express the essence of Biology 101! Generally speaking, these two facts form the foundation for eros love, the love formed between two individuals coming together as one in the commitment of holy matrimony.

Eros love seems simple to understand but challenging to navigate. Eros is what makes your palms sweaty, your eyes sparkle, and your mouth ache from smiling so much when you find another person attractive and feel drawn to them. This kind of love may seem purely biological and physical at first glance, but the sexual component is more of an expression of eros love than its essence. This is why the interplay of physical sensations and arousals and emotions must be broken down into the biological and neurological factors at work. Otherwise, physical and sexual expressions would simply be a matter of choice based on pleasure and procreation. But God made us for eros love in ways that transcend just its physical expression.

Which is why we make distinctions between attraction and lust—and the subsequent attachments made between two people sharing eros love. Dr. Helen Fisher at Rutgers University explains that these aspects of love—attraction, lust, and attachment[3]—can overlap, though each category is distinct with its own hormone cocktail and physical attributes. Each one reflects a different dimension of eros but fails to define it singularly.

Attraction may seem to be based on your sensory impressions of another person or emotions that spring from your heart. The reality, though, is that attraction occurs when your sensory data activates the reward center of your brain, including the hypothalamus, which releases dopamine and norepinephrine—chemicals well-known for the high they produce. Yes, these are the same brain chemicals triggered by certain substances and pharmaceuticals, the kind that elevate your mood, energize your body, and excite your emotions.[4]

So when you're attracted to someone, you usually experience the same physical and neurological lift that occurs from taking drugs like cocaine, meth, and amphetamines. You may feel your pulse race, struggle to focus, and lose your appetite for food. Curiously enough, these bodily changes are similar to those triggered by our human fight-or-flight response that occurs when we're stressed, endangered, or alerted to the unexpected.

Makes sense, doesn't it? Being attracted to someone, including those feelings and sensations we often label as part of "falling in love," causes your body and brain to feel an elevation and acceleration as well as to prepare for imminent danger and disruption. When we separate our rational judgment and spiritual discernment from the attraction equation, we usually end up sliding into lust.

DANGER ZONES

Lust, similarly, operates in ways that leave us feeling out of control and nearly powerless to our carnal cravings. Fueled mostly by the desire for sexual gratification, lust is genetically incorporated into us in order to reproduce and keep our species alive. This drive is shared by almost all living organisms and explains their ability to sustain ongoing life cycles. When sexual arousal begins, the body wants to follow its natural design for satisfying release leading to reproduction.

Like attraction, lust also activates the reward center of our brains, particularly the hypothalamus again—only the reproductive urge stimulates the hormones testosterone and estrogen. You may have learned that these hormones are uniquely male and female, but both are at work in all human bodies. Testosterone ignites the libido in both men and women, while estrogen increases women's desire for sex during ovulation, when their bodies are most likely to conceive.[5]

While lust and attraction may sound like biological forces that overwhelm the body and send a person out of control, we always maintain our ability to choose our behaviors. These choices are often reinforced by the third kind of love, *attachment*, which explains why we want to build relationships with particular individuals in our lives. Attachment is important for sustaining a romantic relationship, but it also determines the quality of virtually all our human relationships—with parents and family, friends and coworkers, social groups and allegiances, cultural identity and ethnicity. Oxytocin and vasopressin are the hormones released as part of attachment.[6]

Because attachment is foundational to the ways we love across all relationships and all kinds of love, we will explore it in more detail in our next chapter. For now, just remember that attachment determines how we connect and bond with one another emotionally, such as desiring to commit to one person and get married, and also physically, as when women breastfeed their babies or parents nurture their newborns.

Attraction, lust, and attachment are all part of eros, but none of them explain the essence of this kind of love. Beyond the biology and neurology, we must turn to the ultimate source of wisdom, the Bible. There we not only find a deeper understanding of eros but see it played out in some of the most dramatic stories of the Old Testament—not only between men and women but between God and His people.

FLESH OF MY FLESH

The reason eros cannot be defined by attraction, lust, and attachment is the same reason human beings are not animals at the mercy of their biological urges. God has given us a mind with which to reason and a will with which to make choices. From a biblical perspective, eros comes down to how we choose to control and direct our bodies and minds based on the guidelines and purposes God has given us in His Word.

While the Greek word *eros* is not specifically used in Scripture, it's implicit in the way certain relationships are described, both literally and figuratively. In the Old Testament eros expresses the intimacy between husband and wife, the physical and sensual and sexual knowing of one another, the union of who they are into a new bond of holy matrimony. This is the sacred kind of relationship we see between Adam and Eve, Abraham and Sarah, Ruth and Boaz, Esther and King Xerxes. This is the sense of union that shares one body: "This is now bone of my bones and flesh of my flesh" (Gen. 2:23).

Most New Testament references to eros celebrate its goodness within a marriage as well as the danger of expressing it immorally. This duality is summed up and contrasted in Hebrews: "Marriage should be honored by all, and the marriage bed kept pure, for God will judge the adulterer and all the sexually immoral" (13:4). In his letter to believers in Corinth, Paul explained both the beauty and the danger of eros in similar fashion:

> Now for the matters you wrote about: "It is good for a man not to have sexual relations with a woman." But since sexual immorality is occurring, each man should have sexual relations with his own wife, and each woman with her own

husband. The husband should fulfill his marital duty to his wife, and likewise the wife to her husband. The wife does not have authority over her own body but yields it to her husband. In the same way, the husband does not have authority over his own body but yields it to his wife. Do not deprive each other except perhaps by mutual consent and for a time, so that you may devote yourselves to prayer. Then come together again so that Satan will not tempt you because of your lack of self-control. (1 Corinthians 7:1–5)

Note here that "duty" and "authority" refer to the mutual, consensual giving of oneself to their beloved—not having it taken forcibly or against one's will. This passage has often been misinterpreted and misused to enforce sexual submission, which goes against the very essence of what true eros—and godly love—is all about. Notice, too, Paul's emphasis on maintaining self-control in order to resist temptations from the enemy. As you and I know too well, our sexuality is often a minefield where Satan loves to sabotage our Christian faith.

In addition to literal references to eros within marriage, the Bible also reveals how God chose this kind of love as a metaphor for the relationship He has with His people. Christ is called the Bridegroom and the church is His holy bride (see John 3:29, Luke 5:34, 2 Cor. 11:2, and Rev. 19:7, to name a few). One of the most beautiful and poetic usages of this metaphor, however, emerges in the Old Testament book known as the Song of Songs, sometimes called the Song of Solomon.

In this sensual, romantic book of poetry, King Solomon and his bride exchange passionate discourse that includes but also transcends their physical love and adoration for one another. In their exchange we see the wholesome delight God intends between husband and wife as well as an expression of God's devoted passion for those He calls His beloved:

> Let him kiss me with the kisses of his mouth—
>> for your love is more delightful than wine.
> Pleasing is the fragrance of your perfumes;
>> your name is like perfume poured out . . .
> We rejoice and delight in you;
>> we will praise your love more than wine. (Song of Songs 1:2–3, 5)

While Song of Songs illustrates an erotic dimension within a loving marriage, it also includes the necessity of the spiritual and emotional aspects of relating. When we love someone as our spouse, we want all of them and want to give all of ourselves to them. Similarly, God has always wanted all of us and gave His Son, Jesus, in order that we might have a personal, intimate relationship with Him. Eros reflects the kind of comprehensive giving and receiving of love that is both quite physical and completely divine.

BEST FRIENDS FOREVER

The way eros emerges in Scripture makes it clear that physical and erotic love is not enough to sustain the commitment of marriage. It requires another kind of love we are all made to give and receive— phileo love. Similar to eros, numerous examples and references to phileo love emerge from both the Old and the New Testaments. In fact, phileo serves as a foundation for the way we interact with those around us—in friendship, connection, cooperation, and solidarity.

While shown in our attitudes to everyone we encounter, phileo is most often associated with friendship. Proverbs warns us that unreliable friends lead to ruin, while a true friend is like family (see 18:24). God even calls Himself a friend to those who are good and honest (see Prov. 3:32). Even more revealing about phileo love, perhaps, are the friendships described between David and Jonathan as well as Ruth and Naomi. Despite interference from Jonathan's father, King Saul, "Jonathan became one in spirit with David, and he loved him as himself" (1 Sam. 18:1). Widowed and left to fend for themselves, Ruth refused to abandon her mother-in-law, promising, "Where you go I will go, and where you stay I will stay. Your people will be my people and your God my God. Where you die I will die, and there I will be buried. May the LORD deal with me, be it ever so severely, if even death separates you and me" (Ruth 1:16–17).

In the New Testament Jesus repeatedly reinforces the significance of phileo love. "Greater love has no one than this: to lay down one's life for one's friends" (John 15:13). He goes on to say that He regards His followers as friends rather than servants because He loves them and has shared His knowledge of His Father with them (see John 15:14–16). Jesus not only enjoyed friendships with His twelve disciples, but also His friendship with Mary, Martha, and their brother, Lazarus, was very important to Him. While grieving Lazarus's death, Jesus called him "our friend" before returning him to life (John 11:11).

What the Bible says about phileo may seem far removed from the way you were made to love others with phileo love, but you only have to reflect on your closest friends to close that gap. Whom do you trust with your heart? When separated, why do you miss those individuals who seem to see you, enjoy you, accept you, and love you despite your flaws and weaknesses? Why do you long to connect with others where you live, work, worship, and play?

That longing is for being known by others for who you truly are, not just who you think others want or need you to be. True phileo love takes risks and dares vulnerability in order to connect at a heart level and not just a people-pleasing, often manipulative level. Which is why you feel lonely so often in the midst of a crowd and feel invisible despite hundreds if not thousands of social media followers and connections. Because you were designed for the same heart connection that united David and Jonathan as well as Ruth and Naomi.

You were made to love others as you love yourself.

TENDERHEARTED

Phileo creates bonds and commitments among people who seemingly have little in common but choose to accept, know, and love one another. Phileo reveals the way love often transcends family, duty, and obligation and relies on our ability to give and receive love without expecting anything in return, which contributes to and overlaps with storge love, the compassionate disposition and loyal commitment to people for whom you feel responsibility.

Similar to the way eros emerges in Scripture, the word *storge* is not actually found in the ancient languages, but it clearly emerges as a conceptual category for familial love. *Storge* comes from the Greek word *philostorgos*, which literally means "tenderly loving." It implicitly carries a sense of the natural tenderness and kindness shown by a parent to a child or by an adult child to an aging parent.

While storge is not directly referenced in the Bible, its antonym, or opposite, is mentioned by Paul in his letter to the Romans (see Rom. 1:31). There, he refers to the godless and wicked people who have ignored the Lord and turned away from Him and His ways.

Paul uses the Greek word *astorgous*, which means "heartless" or "without a tender heart" to conclude, "They are backstabbers, haters of God, insolent, proud, and boastful. They invent new ways of sinning, and they disobey their parents. They refuse to understand, break their promises, are heartless, and have no mercy" (Rom. 1:30–31 NLT).

In contrast then, storge love emerges in the loving, loyal, merciful, kind, and obedient ways someone loves God and their parents. Storge love sacrifices for the love of the family and shows patience, humility, and tenderness. In the Old Testament we see storge between Abraham and Sarah, Noah and his wife and children, and Isaac and Jacob; Joseph shows storge love for his brothers, even after they betray him and sell him into slavery. In the New Testament the love of Joseph for his fiancée-with-child, Mary, exercises storge, as does the love sisters Mary and Martha display for their brother, Lazarus.

God values storge love just as much as the other forms of love. Children are repeatedly instructed to honor, respect, and obey their parents, which God considered important enough to include in His Ten Commandments to the people of Israel (see Exod. 20:12). This kind of familial love also emerges within the family of believers. Jesus explained how spiritual families are just as significant as our families of origin:

> While Jesus was still talking to the crowd, his mother and brothers stood outside, wanting to speak to him. Someone told him, "Your mother and brothers are standing outside, wanting to speak to you."
>
> He replied to him, "Who is my mother, and who are my brothers?" Pointing to his disciples, he said, "Here are my mother and my brothers. For whoever does the will of

my Father in heaven is my brother and sister and mother." (Matthew 12:46–50)

Being part of the family of God goes beyond friendship and results in the kind of loving, enduring relationships that are just as powerful as those we are born into. In the early days of the church, believers united to love one another and to share the gospel of Jesus with all people. We're told they lived communally, selling their property and possessions in order to provide for all those in need. They ate together, prayed together, sang together, and evangelized together (see Acts 2:44–47).

Storge love has broader implications as well—maintaining a tender heart toward God and a respect for those He places in authority—which we will explore in greater detail in chapter 9. For now, keep in mind that storge love emerges in your desire to be part of something bigger than yourself, to have purpose and a mission in life. And to live out that purpose and mission with others who are moving in the same direction.

HOLE IN YOUR HEART

Finally, we come to agape, the basis for all other forms of love. Agape reflects the spiritual longing at the heart of our being to know God and love Him. This longing will not be satisfied by any of the other forms or kinds of love, although we may often try. But the hole in our hearts reflects the spiritual hunger inside us to know and connect with our Creator, our divine Abba Father who loved us enough to send His only Son as a sacrifice for us.

We are born with the capacity to love because He first loved us (see 1 John 4:19) and because we are created in His divine image (see Gen. 1:26–28). Even after we blew it, God's intention to love us and model how to love found another way. When we chose to use God's gift of free will to rebel against Him and His love—He loved us enough to give us the choice—He still refused to give up on us: "But God demonstrates his own love for us in this: While we were still sinners, Christ died for us" (Rom. 5:8).

The Bible is crystal clear in explicitly communicating that there is no human being—past, present, or future—who can earn their way to heaven or have a personal relationship with God without accepting His free gift of salvation through the sacrifice of His Son, Jesus Christ. That's the essence of the gospel, the epitome of love in action!

Without God's presence in our lives, we would still be designed to love—we're still His creation made in His image—but we would be limited by our own selfishness, stubbornness, and silliness. We would love until it got painful and harder than we could bear. We would love until the money ran out or the addiction started or the arrest was made. We would love as best we could until we had nothing left to give and had to walk away in order to survive.

Agape love, however, changes everything. Agape is the power of God's Spirit living in us and empowering us beyond our own abilities, selfish tendencies, and stubborn resistance. Agape, as we will continue to discover, is the ultimate remedy for lazy love in all its forms. When you're securely attached to divine love, you no longer withhold and reserve what you can give to others. You no longer have to feel defensive and guarded, second-guessing others in an attempt to get the love you want without the inflated economy of heartbreak.

Agape energizes you to be the lover God created you to be.

The husband or wife God created you to be.

The mother or father God created you to be.

The brother or sister God created you to be.

The son or daughter God created you to be.

The friend or best friend God created you to be.

The brother or sister in Christ God created you to be.

Agape transforms you into the new creature in Christ you were created by God to be!

STOP SETTLING

We have reviewed an abundance of information and biblical examples. We have made clearer distinctions between one kind of love and another and established differences between eros and phileo, storge and agape. We have embraced the fact that God designed each one of us to know Him and love Him, and to love others as He first loved us. With all of these insights in mind, it should be easier to overcome lazy love, right?

Unfortunately, knowing how God designed us to love isn't enough.

Even as we realize we cannot do it alone and must rely on the Holy Spirit, our hearts can still resist exercise and crave the comfortable. Overcoming lazy love requires more than just scientific knowledge, biblical insight, and experiential wisdom. Defeating lazy love means looking at what's not working within ourselves. Yes, God designed us to love as He has loved us, but frequently our pasts impair our capacity to love.

Somewhere between being made to give love and being made to receive love, a chasm opens, a gap between what we long for and what we can experience, a gulf between our desire to be loved and the reality of others' failures. Left to fester, this span between our potential and our perspective deteriorates our hope, undermines our willingness to risk, and impedes our ability to see others, ourselves, and God clearly.

How do we close this gap?

We look within and begin charting the cracks and fissures in our hearts and invite God's presence into those spaces. We recognize the many false beliefs and harmful patterns we tend to keep repeating and break the spell we're under. We shift our perspective from what we lack to what we have, from the past to the present, and from the now to the not-yet.

It's okay to be anxious or even a little scared.

But do not allow your fears or skepticism to prevent you from all that God has for you.

Because God did not design you with a lazy heart.

Your Creator made you with a heart that's tender, compassionate, gentle, strong, resilient, humble, and passionate. He made you with a heart that's both wild and wondrous, willful and wandering. And no matter how badly you've been hurt or how often you've vowed never to be vulnerable again, you need to be honest with yourself.

If you didn't want more—more capacity to love and to be loved—then you wouldn't have picked up this book.

It's time to explore the cause of your laziness and to discover your true capacity to love.

It's time to stop settling for lazy love.

It's time to experience the love God made you to enjoy.

CHAPTER 3

We Are All Made to Be Loved

One is loved because one is loved. No reason is needed for loving.

—Paulo Coelho

How do you like your steak?" my friend asked.

I could barely see him from behind the steaming, smoking lid of his elaborate grill. The sound of sizzling beef only enhanced the scent wafting my way across the beautiful backyard patio. "Medium!" I called out and then added, "Medium at a minimum or medium well if it's not too well done."

He laughed. "So not rare then?"

"No, sir—definitely not rare!"

Our exchange reminded me of being asked that same question recently in a top-level, Michelin-starred restaurant. Only when I gave the same answer to our waiter, I sensed a slight frown of disapproval, as if he assumed I didn't appreciate the culinary artistry of that particular establishment. I knew all right, knew that I was paying for an exquisite meal that I wanted prepared the way I preferred and enjoyed most based on past experience.

I know it's often customary to trust the chef and allow him or her to make any and all decisions for you. With all due respect, however, I think it can be a license for laziness in the kitchen. Because only a lazy cook would open a restaurant and proclaim, "I don't care who you are or what you like or what allergies you may have. You have to eat and pay for whatever I have decided to cook today." From my experience, a true chef asks you what you want and delights in preparing it exactly to your specifications.

Lazy cooks make it about what's easy, convenient, and amenable for them.

Great chefs make it about what's preferable, delicious, and personalized for you.

Love often works the same way.

We are all made to be loved—but not loved the same way.

Lazy love offers what it wants, the way it wants.

Real love wants to know how to love you the way you want to be loved.

COOKING LESSONS

Rather than stubbornly sticking to our limited menu, we must expand our repertoire and learn to love others in ways that touch them. Just as you might take cooking lessons in order to have more to offer diners, we must learn to love beyond our own limitations. If we fail to realize how lazy love leaves others—and ourselves—lacking, then we miss out on discovering how to love uniquely and personally. Too often we love others in the way we know how to love rather than in the way they need to be loved.

If we are all made to love, the complementary corollary is that we are all made to be loved. The two go together, of course, but that's also where we find the seeds of lazy love. Because the love we initially received in our lives, along with its availability and continuity, remains foundational to our ability to give and receive love the rest of our lives.

Before you dismiss this connection as either obvious or far-reaching, look back on your major relationships—with parents, siblings, close friends, lovers and partners, spouses and exes—and notice what they have in common. You may already have reflected on them and noticed parallels. Or you may be gaining insight into your relational history for the first time.

At some point in our lives, though, we begin to see a pattern—a repetition in our relationships that leaves us feeling disappointed but unsure how to break the cycle. Once we realize the pattern, it seems obvious but nonetheless is troubling. It's hard to believe we keep repeating the same dynamics, the same conversations, the same up-and-down dramas, with the same people or the same kind of people.

INSATIABLE HUNGER

You may have noticed your pattern after a painful breakup. As you sifted through the debris cluttering your broken heart, you saw the clues leading up to the inevitable outcome. You met someone and started hanging out, then seeing each other exclusively. Things seemed good for a while. But from the beginning, you felt desperate and needy. The more you wondered if you loved this person, the more you worked hard to convince yourself that this was the one. Like an attorney making her closing argument again and again, you pressured your partner—directly and indirectly—to prove their love and reassure you.

At first, you told yourself it was just your insecurity lurking. Past relationships had left you wary and guarded, reluctant to trust another person to see you—all of you, not just the pretty Instagram shots posted and the selfies shared—and be capable of loving you. Once the L-word was used, perhaps sooner than you intended to say it, your insecurity grew into doubt and your doubt metastasized into sabotage. Your partner began to be annoyed by your need for constant reassurance, reinforcement, and recognition.

Your incessant texts, questions, and desperate moods became a self-fulfilling prophecy. You felt like you were too much for this person, that you wanted more than they were willing to give, until finally you were proved right. They called you "needy" and "clingy" and challenged you to face your insecurity and commitment to believing that no one could truly know you and actually love you. Whether you acknowledged the truth of their message or not, you knew your secret was out. Your desperate, anxious heart had been exposed, and fresh evidence pointed to the fact that no one was ever going to be enough for you.

You knew you needed love, but the hunger in your heart felt insatiable.

IF YOU LOVE ME, GO AWAY

Perhaps this wasn't a pattern you recognized. Instead, you might have noticed the way your friendships tended to fizzle and fall apart because you were too busy and preoccupied to nurture them, enjoy them, and trust the investment of others in your life. The catalyst for recognizing this cycle might have been the desire to connect with someone at a level deeper than social media or polite small talk could ever touch—only to realize there's no one to turn to.

You might have been facing a health crisis, waiting on the results of a biopsy or CAT scan, and feeling alone in your fear, anxiety, and uncertainty. You could have been dealing with issues regarding an adult child or a loved one's battle with addiction. You didn't like holding the weight of your worries by yourself, but confiding in a friend felt like it would be revealing weakness, vulnerability, and more of your true self than you dared to reveal.

So you hardened your resolve to rely on no one but yourself. You refused to be seen as needy, as someone who required others in order to feel okay. You had gotten this far by yourself and believed somehow you would deal with things on your own. You allowed this self-reliant defense system to barricade your heart behind a facade of fine: "I'm just fine. Thanks for asking. How about you?" Soon you didn't want to enjoy even casual interactions with friends—meeting for coffee, shopping together, dining after work, chatting at church. You were always "too busy" and had "other plans."

You might not identify with either of those patterns, but instead see strains of both in the way you interact with those closest to you. With your spouse or romantic partner, you feel a definite connection and you care about them deeply. Things between you seem strong and solid until you start to feel emotionally claustrophobic and need "some space." Assuming the other person understands and gives you a bit of room and independence, you soon start feeling afraid of losing them. So you recommit and try to move toward them in a loving, vulnerable stance once again.

Or perhaps the dynamic of your relationship is more volatile, with frequent conflicts followed by making up. But each time you face a problem, even when resolved amicably, you internally withdraw. You're afraid of relying on this person too much, so you think it would be better to be the first to back away before they have a greater power to hurt you. Rather than assuming conflicts are natural and healthy for all relationships, you view them as indicators of inevitability, certain that eventually you will be alone once again.

This kind of push-pull has variations, but the outcome is almost always the same—distance, disruption, disappointment, divorce. You get close and start to feel seen and loved and then back away and put distance between the two of you. You then start missing the other person, worrying that they will find someone else or longing for love, so you reapproach until the next time you back away. Sooner or later, though, your partner gets tired of this romantic roller-coaster ride and refuses to stay onboard.

Yes, the tempo of this temperamental tango might vary, but the dance steps are always the same. Sooner or later, others begin to get your mixed message: "Please love me but go away!"

SECURE ATTACHMENT

Regardless of which pattern you have recognized before or which variations apply, you likely wonder why this happens time and again. You cannot deny that you want to be loved, really loved, for who you truly are and not just who others want you to be. And yet you feel stuck, orbiting the same relational rotation until you wonder if you will ever be loved the way you want and deserve to be loved.

If you've ever felt this way, then you need to know two important facts. First, you are most definitely not alone. Just as human beings are made in God's image and made to love, we are also made to be loved. We are born helpless and dependent so that we can experience what it means to be loved just for showing up. Unfortunately, the choices, failures, addictions, and abandonment of others often means we fail to get what we were made to receive. Which in turn sets us up to carry these wounds inside.

Perhaps your father left when you were very young and you never had a relationship with him. Or your mother battled an addiction that forced her to leave you in the care of others, causing you to wonder if her problem was somehow your fault. Of course it wasn't, but children often assume responsibility rather than face the painful truth of their parents' shortcomings. You might have been bullied and unable to attach to peers and friends the way your heart longed to be known. You may have struggled to belong and wondered why no one seemed to want you included the way you wanted to be wanted.

Both the big wounds and the small slights caused a breach in your capacity to love because of how you were not loved as God intended you to be. These deficits left you lacking and longing for something to comfort and compensate for the past. So you ended up in a cycle of dating men who abandoned you, repeating what you experienced with your father as a child when he walked out on you and your mom. Or the pain of past losses may have felt so intensely painful that you turned to alcohol or drugs, porn or online gambling, shopping or social media approval to take you out of that overwhelming sense of emptiness and ache.

Regardless of our childhood and upbringing, we all have some scars from not being loved perfectly. There are no perfect relationships, and all the imperfections can sometimes have a cumulative impact. So the way you respond to being loved can be traced back to when you first entered this world.

As newborns, we are each born into a relational context that's already in motion. No matter how much your parents loved you and wanted to care for you, they had their own limitations, with some being more severe than others. Infants are basically helpless and depend on their parents or caregivers to meet their needs. As intelligent, sentient beings, babies also learn quickly how, when, and if their needs are getting met.

This is the basic foundation for what psychologists often call *human attachment*.

John Bowlby is the pioneering practitioner often associated with shaping what's known as attachment theory. Bowlby had been trained in classic psychoanalysis but also studied child psychiatry and developmental psychology. Once he began working in a psychiatric hospital, Bowlby wondered why different children could have such distinct and varied relational styles. His observations challenged the emphasis on the internal, emotional, and biological factors shaping personality and caused him to focus on external variables such as home environment, styles of parenting, and socioeconomic needs.[1]

By the 1950s Bowlby zeroed in on mother-child separation issues, building on the work of others such as Konrad Lorenz, and eventually concluded that babies rely on their mothers not only for food but for emotional security in maintaining their connection. Others began to reach similar conclusions and devised studies to test their hypothesis, including some that involved separating toddlers from their mothers in various situations. Today, attachment theory has become a highly regarded and respected area of therapeutic study and treatment. It has become widely known and mainstreamed as a way of growing in self-awareness and creating stronger relationships.[2]

Which brings us to the four main styles of attachment most experts now recognize: secure attachment, anxious attachment, avoidant attachment, and ambivalent attachment. Secure attachment occurs when a baby experiences a mother who is attentive, reliable, soothing, and sustaining. While not perfect, secure attachments reflect the bond we were made to enjoy with parents who are physically, emotionally, and psychologically equipped for caregiving. Such parenting conveys a sense of constancy, consistency, connection, and comfort. Their attention and responsiveness to a baby's needs—for food, for touch, for cleanliness when diapers need changing—signal their love and devotion to their dependent little one. When the mother and child are separated, the baby expresses distress but is quickly soothed and contented almost immediately when reunited.

Secure attachment ensures that infants grow into healthy children who know they are loved and cherished. They trust their parents to provide not only the material essentials for them but also the emotional foundation for maturation into adulthood. Securely attached adults know how to build relationships at a healthy pace, gradually building trust and maintaining boundaries. They experience the ability to give and receive love by balancing their individual needs and autonomy with their connections to others.

TOO MUCH AND NEVER ENOUGH

Secure attachments are what we are all born craving, but not necessarily what we experience. While attachments begin in infancy, they continue throughout a child's life, both reinforcing and challenging the conclusions the child formed early on instinctively. Which leads to less-than-secure attachment styles, including anxious attachment. This style develops when a child's nervous system is extra-sensitive or easily activated. As babies they may be fussy or difficult to comfort at times. If they do not receive the extra attention and reassurance they need, they may become overly afraid their parents will not be there for them or meet their needs.

As children with anxious attachment mature, they are often shy, clingy, or need to be with parents, siblings, or close friends at all times. Their worst fear is being abandoned or having the source of their security, whomever that may be, fail to provide for their needs. In adulthood these individuals often fall into codependency, needing to be part of a couple to the point of sacrificing their independence and healthy boundaries. They may seem overly emotional and need constant reassurance that their partner or spouse loves them and will be there for them. Sometimes their anxiety about the relationship leads to what they fear most—being left alone.

Avoidant attachment, on the other hand, occurs in babies who are more self-soothing and content without being held or touched by their parents. They might also have parents who aren't fully attentive, leaving them to conclude that they must rely on themselves. As they mature they can be less emotional and more rational, self-reliant and compliant, sidestepping the need to bond with peers or win their approval. They may be well-liked and appreciated but not well-known below surface impressions.

Once adults, they struggle to be vulnerable and intimate with even those closest to them. They view healthy needs as inherently dangerous since they could lead to depending on others who can't be trusted or aren't reliable. Avoidant attachment causes people to remain at arm's length, longing for the love they could have if they would risk being known and receiving what others want to give them.

The final attachment style, often called ambivalent or anxious-ambivalent, features aspects of both anxious and avoidant styles. Ambivalence develops when an infant, and later a child, concludes that their needs are frequently met by their parents or caregivers but not consistently. They know they need their parents' love but resist trusting it because of the pain when their needs go unmet.

As adults, those people with an ambivalent attachment style often send mixed signals and fall into the push-pull style of relating. They know they need love and want to give and receive it with their spouse, families, and friends. But they also know that people are not always dependable; they can disappoint and sometimes betray them. So ambivalence sets in and they take one step toward the love offered to them but then take two steps back.

Lazy love becomes the new normal—unless we learn to break old patterns and experience love the way we were designed to be loved.

THIRST TRAP

Before we talk about how to move beyond lazy love and form healthier, more secure attachments as adults, I want to pause for a moment and consider our human desire to be loved from another perspective—God's perspective. When our needs for love are not met, we often attempt to fill them ourselves or deny them altogether by hardening our hearts. Tilting in either extreme direction, we miss out on the way God can heal us and use our relationships to reveal more of who He is and His love for us.

In the last chapter we explored how we are created in God's image as social, relational beings designed to love as He has loved us. But now I want to consider how our desire for love can become overshadowed by our fears, doubts, uncertainties, and disappointments—unless we allow God to create the ultimate secure attachment. Doing so requires us to get in touch with our soul's deepest thirst, a fundamental longing for love from a divine source, a thirst trap like no other.

Now, you're probably familiar with the kind of thirst traps you find online these days—sexy pics or flirty memes designed to attract viewers and tease their senses. These thirst traps are often used as click-bait to promote various products—cosmetics and perfume, clothing and jewelry, cars and lifestyles—or celebrity brands. But these thirst traps are not the first to compare our longing for connection to our need for water. The Bible made that comparison thousands of years ago!

In one of His most scandalous encounters, Jesus dared to engage with a woman whose reputation was less than sterling. He not only bucked cultural norms and talked to her respectfully—He saw straight into her heart. Their meeting occurred when Jesus and His disciples were returning to Galilee from Judea (see John 4:1–3). Their route crossed into Samaria, and specifically the town of Sychar, famous historically because Jacob gifted his favorite son, Joseph, land there (see John 4:5).

Traveling through this place, Jesus stopped to rest around noon at a watering hole called Jacob's well (see John 4:6). A local woman who was there to fill her water jugs then learned how our souls need water just as much as our bodies:

When a Samaritan woman came to draw water, Jesus said to her, "Will you give me a drink?" (His disciples had gone into the town to buy food.) The Samaritan woman said to him, "You are a Jew and I am a Samaritan woman. How can you ask me for a drink?" (For Jews do not associate with Samaritans.) Jesus answered her, "If you knew the gift of God and who it is that asks you for a drink, you would have asked him and he would have given you living water."

"Sir," the woman said, "you have nothing to draw with and the well is deep. Where can you get this living water? Are you greater than our father Jacob, who gave us the well and drank from it himself, as did also his sons and his livestock?" Jesus answered, "Everyone who drinks this water will be thirsty again, but whoever drinks the water I give them will never thirst. Indeed, the water I give them will become in them a spring of water welling up to eternal life."

The woman said to him, "Sir, give me this water so that I won't get thirsty and have to keep coming here to draw water." He told her, "Go, call your husband and come back." "I have no husband," she replied. Jesus said to her, "You are right when you say you have no husband. The fact is, you have had five husbands, and the man you now have is not your husband. What you have just said is quite true." (John 4:7–18)

DRINKING UP THE DIVINE

Jesus showed no concern or trepidation about talking to this Samaritan woman, who was considered unclean and ungodly by the majority of Jews at that time. So when Jesus asked her for a drink of water, He immediately grabbed her attention. Who was this Jewish stranger to ask her of all people for anything? Such a request, let alone if she honored it, violated Jewish religious customs, not to mention cultural stereotypes.

Sharing her confusion with the man requesting a drink, the woman discovered they were talking about more than one kind of thirst. Jesus used their encounter to create a perfect metaphor for the unquenchable longing in this woman's life, saying in essence: "If you knew who I am, you would ask Me for the only thing that can fill the longing in your thirsty soul—living water."

The way Jesus switched from physical to spiritual thirst likely confused the Samaritan woman even more. She asked how He could give her a drink of water without any kind of container. Indirectly moving toward Christ's meaning, she drew on the Jewish historical significance of their location. Basically, she said, "Knowing where we are, are You greater than our forefather Jacob?"

Jesus then explained Himself and made His meaning clear. A drink of water from Jacob's well would provide hydration to relieve physical thirst, but the water He offered could quench a greater, seemingly insatiable thirst inside her heart.

Who wouldn't want that kind of water, right? So the Samaritan woman requested this living water offered by this mysterious stranger. Drinking it, she assumed she would not have to keep returning there to draw her daily supply of water. In other words, she still wasn't quite realizing what Jesus was offering—so Jesus took a different, more personal, approach. He told her to go and get her husband, to which she replied she didn't have a husband.

Jesus then made His meaning as clear as the cool water drawn from the well: "You are right when you say you have no husband. The fact is, you have had five husbands, and the man you now have is not your husband. What you have just said is quite true" (John 4:17–18). Jesus clearly knew everything about her!

Notice that He dropped this revelation with kindness and respect, though. There was no accusation or condemnation, no name-calling or shaming delivery, no sordid details or religious judgment. Jesus just spoke the truth to her, revealing evidence that the thirst inside her would never be satisfied by husbands and lovers. Instead of drinking water drawn from down in the well, it was time for her to quench her thirst by drinking up from the divine.

WELLSPRING OF LOVE

Based on His intimate knowledge of her life, the Samaritan woman assumed Jesus must be a prophet. Jesus told her she was close but not quite there, and then it hit her:

The woman said, "I know that Messiah" (called Christ) "is coming. When he comes, he will explain everything to us."

Then Jesus declared, "I, the one speaking to you—I am he." Just then his disciples returned and were surprised to find him talking with a woman. But no one asked, "What do you want?" or "Why are you talking with her?" Then, leaving her water jar, the woman went back to the town and said to the people, "Come, see a man who told me everything I ever did. Could this be the Messiah?" They came out of the town and made their way toward him . . . Many of the Samaritans from that town believed in him because of the woman's testimony, "He told me everything I ever did." (John 4:25–30, 39)

Jesus allowed this woman to reach her own conclusion about His identity before confirming Himself as the Messiah. In relating to her in a human way first, He allowed her to be seen and known in ways she probably had never experienced before—certainly not by the previous men in her life. This roundabout way of discovery also reinforced the grace Jesus offered her rather than any sense of shame or condemnation.

When the disciples caught up with Jesus and found Him chatting with someone culturally inappropriate, they probably wondered what was going on. To their credit, however, they knew Jesus well enough by that time not to question Him or His ways, which John points out. The ways of God are clearly not the ways of humans.

The Samaritan woman was then so excited to run and tell her friends and neighbors about her encounter with the Messiah that she forgot to grab her water jug, leaving it at the well. Tasting the living water, the fresh, spring-fed spiritual water of Christ, this woman was changed. She discovered a wellspring that would never run dry and simply had to share it. She received the love she had been created to receive like never before in her life. Her excitement must have impressed everyone she knew because they approached Jesus and also believed in Him.

We are offered the same living water today.

We don't have to return to online thirst traps, reality romance shows, or app-triggered hookups to quench the deepest longing in our hearts. Jesus knows everything you've done and everyone you've done it with. He knows how you have tried to find water in a desert of mishandled pain and misdirected longing. But now He offers you your fill from the fount of every blessing, the eternal wellspring of heaven. "I have come that they may have life, and have it to the full," Jesus told His followers (John 10:10). And His offer to them—along with the Samaritan woman at the well—remains the same for us today.

FOUNT OF EVERY BLESSING

The woman at the well reminds me of a very different scene in the Old Testament. After Moses led the Israelites out of bondage in Egypt, they wandered in the desert and became parched to the point of death (see Exod. 17:1–7). They turned on Moses and basically accused God of leading them out of the fire and into the frying pan. Without water, they knew they would die—their animals, crops, everything needed water to live. Not coincidentally, without love human beings will also die, whether spiritually or physically or both.

In response, Moses asked God what to do and was instructed to go and strike the rock in front of Mount Sinai, using the same staff that had parted the torrential waters of the Red Sea earlier. The power that had facilitated water being held back would now produce water seemingly out of the least likely place—a rocky spot in the desert. Moses obeyed, water gushed from the rock, and thirsty people quenched dry throats and terrified spirits.

Obviously, God knew the Israelites needed water to survive and planned to provide it. But He also wanted them to depend on Him, to trust Him, to look to Him for a secure attachment rather than their own abilities. The psalmist writes, "As the deer pants for streams of water, so my soul pants for you, my God. My soul thirsts for God, for the living God" (Ps. 42:1–2).

Our Creator made us to be loved and to love. But He also gave us the gift of free will, which means that those needs and how they're met by other humans often get derailed from what God intended and designed us to experience. Regardless of how much our parents, grandparents, caregivers, and families loved us, they had their own weaknesses, flaws, and thirsty holes in their hearts. They likely tried to love us as best they could, which simply wasn't enough to fill us up.

Therefore, we carry into adulthood the consequences of how we received, or lacked, the love we needed. But now we have a choice. We are no longer infants, toddlers, or children. We are adults capable of shepherding our hearts' desires by looking to the ultimate source of love, the Good Shepherd of our souls. By becoming more self-aware of our needs, we can spot recurring patterns and break destructive cycles. We can turn to God for the foundation of love upon which all our other capacities to love are built.

Only in Him can you receive the unconditional love you long for.

Through the power of agape love, you are then liberated to love others.

Empowered by agape, you can overcome the threats poisoning your relationships with lazy love.

THREAT #1

Withholding Your Self due to Lack of Agape

This is how God showed his love among us:
He sent his one and only Son into the world that
we might live through him. This is love: not that
we loved God, but that he loved us and sent his
Son as an atoning sacrifice for our sins…
This is how we know that we live in him
and he in us: He has given us of his Spirit.

1 JOHN 4:9-10, 13

Agape is something of the understanding,
creative, redemptive goodwill for all men.
It is a love that seeks nothing in return.
It is an overflowing love; it's what theologians
would call the love of God working in the lives
of men. And when you rise to love on this level,
you begin to love men, not because they
are likable, but because God loves them.

MARTIN LUTHER KING JR.

CHAPTER 4

The Love of the Father

Many who say "Our Father" on Sunday spend the rest of the week acting like orphans.

—Author Unknown

When I turned twelve, I asked my mother for a gift that cost nothing but risked everything. Pleading with my eyes, I asked, "Who is my father? What's his name?" I said the words "father" and "name" slowly, tentatively, as if even daring to request such highly classified information would set off emergency alarms. I had asked her many times before, and she had always dismissed my query or evaded answering, which left me wondering if my dad was someone important, a professional athlete maybe, or the other extreme, a criminal or someone incapable of responsibly loving his children.

This time felt different, though. Perhaps it was the growth spurt heralding me into adolescence so that I was taller than her. More likely, it was Mom's awareness that I was asking for more than a name—I needed to know where I came from, who I came from, who had made me. Whatever the reason, she sat across from me at our small kitchen table and whispered a familiar name. It turned out that I had known my father for many years. Because the name she uttered belonged to the pastor of our church.

I knew without a doubt she was telling the truth. And my mind immediately ran into a brick wall of confusion about the implications. On one hand, I was relieved and excited. My father was a man of God, a gifted preacher and respected community leader. He was handsome and had the kind of charm and charisma that drew people to him. I could even see my resemblance to him now that I knew the genetic mirror I was gazing into.

On the other hand, I was angry and confused. Knowing all the positive qualities my father possessed, why was he not part of my life? I was old enough to know the answer to that question, especially considering his role as pastor and community leader. The fact that he had a wife, and children with her, only ignited more resentment. While unable to articulate my pain, I felt the weight of his shame crush my hopes for experiencing the love I longed to receive from a father.

THE TRUTH HURTS

My mind and my heart raced to see which could process my mother's revelation first. My heart easily won because my thoughts crumbled in contradictions and disbelief. My mother watched me carefully, and I could tell she was second-guessing her decision to tell me the truth. Based on her demeanor when she whispered my father's name, though, I sensed none of the angry resentment bubbling inside my shaken soul.

Perhaps it was that edge of bitterness that pierced my pride and compelled me to ask the man himself to confirm my mom's disclosure. It wasn't that I doubted her; I simply wanted to look him in the eyes and hear his response. So I mustered my courage with determination and lingered after church the following Sunday morning. My intention had nothing to do with trying to expose or embarrass this man; I simply wanted confirmation and collaboration of what my mother had shared. Waiting for my turn to shake the pastor's hand, I leaned in and said, "Pastor, I have a question for you."

Assuming it had to do with the sermon or Scripture or something related to his pastoral duties, he smiled and replied, "I'll be happy to help you if I can, Keion."

"Are you my father?" My voice grew shaky as tears pooled in my eyes. To his credit, he held my gaze and said, "Let's talk in my office in five minutes, okay? Let me finish here and then we'll talk."

I nodded as he gently ushered me forward and shifted back into smiling pastoral mode for the next congregant. Numb and detached from my feelings, I made a beeline straight to the back of the church to his office. Sure enough, within just a few minutes he approached and led me into his office, shutting the door behind us. He motioned for me to sit in the chair across from him and wasted no time hedging or dodging the truth.

"Yes, Keion, I am your father."

Our eyes remained locked as I tried to peer into this man's soul, searching for answers to how he could be my father and not be in my life. How he could be a pastor, a man of God, a follower of Jesus, and shirk his responsibility for loving, guiding, and nurturing his son.

"I need this . . . to stay between us . . . I'm sorry, but I don't expect you to understand . . ."

"I understand." I nodded and repeated myself: "Yes, sir, I understand."

I understood all too well how my mother had wanted to protect me, how my ignorance had buffered my heart from the raw ache I felt leaving my father's office that day. Up until then I had always tried to keep my emotions in check, holding back my tears or making sure no one else ever saw them. But that Sunday, I no longer cared who saw the rivers flooding down my face. I had always heard that real men don't cry, but I suddenly realized that I had just left my childhood behind and the only thing I could do was cry. Because knowing my father's identity and yet being unable to be acknowledged and loved as his son cut me deeper than not knowing ever had.

THE GOD FATHER

Perhaps you grew up with an amazing father—and I pray that you did. Your dad may have been a constant, loving, reassuring presence throughout your life. There for you when you needed him, to offer comfort and security, protection and provision, wisdom and guidance. But even if your father was that and more, he still falls short of the way God fathers us as His children. No father is perfect, and most people have some level of disappointment or woundedness from their relationship with him. What is yours?

You can imagine how discovering my father's identity, on top of the impact his absence had already carved into my life, affected my view of God. I was raised in the church—the same one I now knew was pastored by my father—and witnessed my mother's faith sustain her as a single woman raising my sisters and me. She kept our heads above water and food on our table by doing whatever was necessary, which included working at the Taco Bell a few miles from our apartment for minimum wage. No matter how hard our circumstances, she persevered with patience and quiet strength, trusting God to provide for us and to meet us right where we were.

Now that I knew the same secret she lived with, I admired her faith all the more. But I also resented her ability to trust God in the midst of such shameful secrecy. And the fact that God was so often called our heavenly Father only made matters worse for me. Looking back with more clarity and maturity, I see the one-two punch pummeling my heart more clearly. The first punch was simply the ache inside me for the father I never had, the one who was never there at my ball games, never there to protect me with the security of his presence, never there to usher me into manhood.

The second blow resulted from the sense of abandonment and rejection I felt personally now that I knew my father could have been involved in my life but chose his reputation instead. My heart has softened with forgiveness over the years, but at that time, just as I was entering the uncertainty of adolescence, I could not fathom how he could ignore my existence, how he could live with himself, how he could represent God and preach the gospel.

The result of this massive father-wound clouded my perception of God for many years. Either God was absent and unknown, distant and detached from the details of my daily life, or else He was cruel and unknowable, a harsh Father claiming He wanted a relationship with me but refusing to show up in the ways I needed a father to show up. Regardless of how I viewed Him, I concluded that if God was a father in any way, shape, or form similar to my earthly father, then I wanted nothing to do with Him.

I used my father's absence as an excuse for resisting God and for abandoning myself. I assumed that if I wasn't worth enough for my dad to want to love and get to know me, then why would anyone else? Then why should I? I allowed my wound to fester into a bitter poison that I spewed whenever anyone dared to see my pain or tried to love me.

I justified my hard-hearted stance by telling myself that this was the reality I had to accept, the pain I had to learn to bury deep inside me. Only later, as I began making bad choices and taking reckless chances, would I realize the truth: I had no connection to a major part of myself—my father—and the wound left a hole in my heart, a chronic ache that I refused to face with compassion or grace. And because of this wound, I refused to question my negative perceptions of God.

Until I could no longer resist the tenderness of my Father's love.

GOOD GIFTS

What does my struggle to view God accurately have to do with His agape love for all of His children? Everything! Agape love is unmerited, unconditional, and undeserved. It is the essence of who God is. And the closest we can come to grasping and knowing Him is as our heavenly Father. In order to improve our vision, however, we must be willing to see beyond our relationship with our earthly father. As my experience testifies, sometimes that's harder than we want it to be.

Because no matter how wonderful, loving, and attentive our earthly father may have been, he is still human and imperfect. And if he wasn't there, or was angry or abusive, then we often experience greater challenges to seeing who God really is. But just because we have human baggage with our biological dads doesn't mean that we can't learn to release it, experience healing, and take a fresh look at God as our Father.

Sometimes loving someone else helps you see more clearly how much God loves you. I realized this once I became a father myself. Experiencing the overflowing love for my daughter, I marveled at how much more God must love me and all of His children. As she grew up I realized that no matter what she did, whether she pleased me with her choices or disappointed me with them, I would love her just the same.

My love for her was not conditional on how well she behaved, acted, or performed. So if I could feel this way, then how much more God must love us despite knowing all our flaws, faults, and failures. Jesus said, "Which of you, if your son asks for bread, will give him a stone? Or if he asks for a fish will give him a snake?" Christ then answers his rhetorical, almost comical, question: "If you, then, though you are evil, know how to give good gifts to your children, how much more will your Father in heaven give good gifts to those who ask him!" (see Matt. 7:9–11).

Despite my rebellious choices and resistance to believing God could love me as the Father I never had, He refused to give up on me. Now I realize that this divine persistence is fundamental to His nature. "Though my father and mother forsake me," the psalmist writes, "the LORD will receive me" (Ps. 27:10). God is not merely a better version of our earthly father—He is our perfect heavenly Father. He reveals Himself as our Father in numerous ways, but perhaps we learn more about God's Father-heart by focusing on His Son, Jesus.

Almost everyone knows the familiar truth of John 3:16: "For God so loved the world that He gave His only begotten Son, that whoever believes in Him should not perish but have everlasting life" (NKJV). But there's more to this good news: God not only gave us His Son to save us from our sins—He gave us His Son to show us more of who He is and how much He loves us. Consider how it is summed up here by the author of Hebrews:

> In the past God spoke to our ancestors through the prophets at many times and in various ways, but in these last days

he has spoken to us by his Son, whom he appointed heir of all things, and through whom also he made the universe. The Son is the radiance of God's glory and the exact representation of his being, sustaining all things by his powerful word. (1:1–3)

LIKE FATHER, LIKE SON

You may recall that the people of Israel struggled with their perception of God just as much as we do. Even after God delivered them from their bondage in Egypt, they still complained, doubted, and rebelled against Him—to the point of worshipping pagan gods or idols of their own making. Then, through His prophets, God made it clear He was going to do something radical: reveal Himself in human form through His Son, Jesus Christ. Jesus, as the Messiah, became the perfect sacrifice so that our sins could be forgiven once and for all.

Through His life on earth—healing and teaching and performing miracles and preaching the gospel of God's grace—Jesus radiated with God's glory, His divine essence and character. As the radiance of God's glory, Christ directly expressed how God wants to be known—as our Father! Not just as an earthly father but as a holy, perfect Papa, an Abba Father who invites His children to climb into His arms and experience His love, acceptance, comfort, and power. When Christ's disciples asked Him to teach them to pray, Jesus instructed them to begin with "Our Father which art in heaven" (Matt. 6:9 KJV).

This instruction was not an isolated incident. Jesus repeatedly referred to God not only as His Father, but as our Father. In fact, we find Jesus referring to God as Father more than 180 times in the four Gospels, the reference He used more than any other. Jesus also made it clear how we as His followers can relate to God as our Father: "I am the way and the truth and the life. No one comes to the Father except through me" (John 14:6). Just to make sure we don't miss His point, Jesus added, "Anyone who has seen me has seen the Father" (John 14:9). Simply put, we can know God by accepting the free gift of salvation through Jesus. And we can relate to God as a Father who loves us lavishly and unconditionally.

A Father who refuses to abandon or forsake us.

A Father who delights in us and blesses us.

A Father who will not let us go no matter how far we may stray.

Perhaps because we sometimes work so hard to distance ourselves from God as our Father, He emphasizes throughout His Word that nothing can separate us from Him. Not our lies, our secret addictions, our teenage indiscretions, our harsh words, our selfish betrayals, or our rebellious hearts. Jesus made this more than clear through one of His favorite methods—by telling a story, a parable. Only to make this point, He told three variations of the same theme.

I think He wants to be sure we get it!

LAVISH LOVE

Jesus wants to be sure His followers know His Father for who He truly is—not who they may assume, expect, or anticipate based on their own experiences. Because God is our perfect Father! He pursues us with relentless love—even when we're not aware of it, don't feel His love the way we want, or run away from Him. As Jesus' three parables reveal, our heavenly Father's loving pursuit of us knows no limits.

The context of Jesus' three-tiered approach included a mix of people for Him and against Him. We're told tax collectors, who were some of the most notoriously corrupt people of that day, and sinners had gathered to hear what Jesus had to say. But Jesus' interaction with such people did not sit well with the Jewish religious leaders, who muttered, "This man welcomes sinners and eats with them" (Luke 15:2). In other words, "Who does He think He is?"

Acutely aware of His audience, Jesus then told them a parable about a shepherd with a hundred sheep. When one of them goes missing, the shepherd leaves the ninety-nine in the pasture and goes looking until he finds the lost lamb. When he finds it, he rejoices and carries it home on his shoulders. The shepherd then informs his friends and neighbors, inviting them to celebrate with him. And just so no one missed the point, Jesus concluded, "I tell you that in the same way there will be more rejoicing in heaven over one sinner who repents than over ninety-nine righteous persons who do not need to repent" (Luke 15:7).

Jesus then proceeded to tell a second story. This time the lost item is one of a woman's ten coins in her possession. Upon realizing she has lost one of them, she wastes no time but immediately lights her lamp and sweeps the house and searches until she finds it. Like the diligent shepherd, this woman invites her friends and neighbors to rejoice with her. "In the same way," Jesus explained, "I tell you, there is rejoicing in the presence of the angels of God over one sinner who repents" (Luke 15:10).

The third and final parable may be the most well-known and the most poignant. Instead of a lost sheep or lost coin, it's a father's younger son who loses himself. The young man demands his inheritance—before his father has died, mind you—and proceeds to leave home on a whirlwind tour of sensual pleasures. Faster than a tourist wastes money in Vegas, this young man lost all he had and found himself feeding pigs—and envying the scraps of food they were enjoying. Then it finally hit him—what he had had and taken for granted:

> When he came to his senses, he said, "How many of my father's hired servants have food to spare, and here I am starving to death! I will set out and go back to my father and say to him: Father, I have sinned against heaven and against you. I am no longer worthy to be called your son; make me like one of your hired servants." So he got up and went to his father. (Luke 15:17–20)

Notice that this young man realized his father was a good man, a reasonable and kind man. Surely, knowing this about his father, the younger son could return home and at least be treated like one of the servants. So swallowing his pride, which wasn't easy on an empty stomach, this poorer but wiser son made his way back home. But what he experienced was not what he expected!

> But while he was still a long way off, his father saw him and was filled with compassion for him; he ran to his son, threw his arms around him and kissed him.
>
> The son said to him, "Father, I have sinned against heaven and against you. I am no longer worthy to be called your son."
>
> But the father said to his servants, "Quick! Bring the best robe and put it on him. Put a ring on his finger and sandals on his feet. Bring the fattened calf and kill it. Let's have a feast and celebrate. For this son of mine was dead and is alive again; he was lost and is found." So they began to celebrate. (Luke 15:20–24)

This picture of God is the Father you never had.

The Father who not only welcomes you home but runs to meet you where you are.

The Father whose agape love for you transcends even the best daddy here on earth.

God's love as your Father is the essence of agape love.

And agape love is the antidote to withholding yourself—one that requires constant connection. When you experience the love of God as a perfect Father, then you no longer ration out your love in relationships with others. You know that even if someone does not love you as you deserve and want to be loved, your lavishly loving Papa always runs to meet you.

EXPAND YOUR CAPACITY

Once I received God's call on my life, I knew I had to come to terms with my father-wound and how it affected other relationships—especially the one with my heavenly Father. I had made progress in both areas but still harbored bitterness and withheld compassion from my earthly father.

Then one day one of my spiritual fathers sensed my need in this area and helped shift my perspective. "Keion, I know you're a father and that you love your children very much, correct?"

"You know me well," I said, uncertain where he was going.

"Then let me ask you this: Would your children ever describe you as perfect? Whether we asked them today or ten years from now, would they ever view you as a perfect father?"

"Well, no one is perfect—only our Lord and Savior, Jesus."

"So you agree that you are not a perfect father?" my mentor said.

He had made his point, but I didn't like his approach one bit. "Okay, I'm never going to be a perfect father. But considering that nobody taught me how to be a father who's involved in his children's lives, I think I'm doing all right. You know the wound I carry because of what I never received from my father."

"Right," he said and nodded. "And I know how hard it remains to forgive your father. But let's think about the story of Mephibosheth for a moment. You remember him, don't you?"

I had always felt a certain kinship with this man mentioned in the Old Testament. Mephibosheth was the son of Jonathan, and therefore the grandson of King Saul. But both his father and his grandfather died in battle with the Philistines when Mephibosheth was only five years old. On top of this devastating news, Mephibosheth was accidentally dropped by his nurse, leaving him crippled for life. With David ascending to the throne of Israel as God's anointed king, Mephibosheth was left a destitute, crippled orphan (see 2 Sam. 4 for the whole story).

"What if," my mentor said, "your father, just like Mephibosheth, was dropped by those entrusted with parenting him? Or what if he, too, was an orphan without the support of a loving father and mother? What if his early wounds affected the rest of his life?"

I immediately felt an ever so slight shift inside my heart. If I was going to begin healing and experience all that God had for me, then I had to choose to forgive my father. I couldn't continue to blame him for every deficit and disappointment in my life. I couldn't continue to withhold compassion and empathy. I recognized the likelihood that those in charge of his development, perhaps especially his own father, had dropped him and caused irreparable damage.

On that day I made a conscious choice to forgive my father, and ever since then I have chosen to forgive and honor him every day.

Despite his failures, misgivings, and the injuries inflicted by those who dropped him, he gave me life. Many would not consider him a good father, but intentionally choosing to honor him continues to empower me in ways I would have missed had I chosen to remain immersed in my pain.

Choosing to forgive my father has drawn me closer to knowing and experiencing the love of my heavenly Father. This is the choice we all make in one way or another. If we refuse to move beyond whatever damage, disappointments, and distractions our earthly fathers caused, then we stand in our own way. When we refuse to open our hearts to God as a perfect Father, we miss out on what we long for most—to know Him and be known by Him. This is the essence of agape love—and the basis for how our hearts love everyone around us.

If you want to overcome lazy love, then you have a choice to make.

You can choose to keep your capacity to love on the same channel and wavelength.

Or you can expand your capacity by loving the way your Father loves.

If you want to love more like your Father loves you, then you likely need to explore what prevents you from experiencing more of His perfect love. The greatest barrier is usually leftover wounding from your relationship with your earthly father. Grieving what you missed from your dad while growing up is never easy or without pain. But it's worth it in order to cleanse your capacity for loving others the same way God loves you.

Without secure attachment to God as your heavenly Father, you will look to other people and other pursuits to fill the longing for divine love inherent in your design. You might acknowledge God, perhaps even try to love Him and serve Him, but you do not trust Him—not with your heart, with your greatest and most painful losses, or with your hopes and grandest dreams. Even worse, you might withdraw completely from God, from church, and from organized religion and any personal practices of faith. Your experiences have taught you that God is not apparently who you thought He was or need Him to be. So you assume you're on your own and act accordingly.

When you're securely attached to your heavenly Father, however, you begin overcoming the threat to settle for lazy love in your relationships. You no longer need to withhold when you are held by the One who loves you most!

CHAPTER 5

The Suffering of the Son

I have found the paradox that if I love until it hurts, then there is no more hurt, but only more love.

—Mother Teresa

Many people not only settle for less than God's best in their relationships—they *suffer* for less as well. They suffer because they refuse to risk. Because they withhold their hearts. Because they grow callous and selfish, indifferent to the price of loving. How you respond to suffering often reveals the health of your relationships.

As a pastor, I encounter the silent suffering of my flock in myriad ways.

I read the pain telegraphed by the trembling shake of a brother's hand, and I know that his Parkinson's condition continues to advance. I peruse the heartache etched across the face of a dear older woman, the delicate lines around her eyes and mouth like those on an ancient map, and I sense her fear, sadness, and uncertainty concerning her adult daughter's battle with drug addiction, and consequently the granddaughter she is now raising.

I study the dark eyes of a young man barely resisting the allure of the gang members in his collapsing community and feel the desperate pleas of a boy searching for a father. It's similar yet distinct from the pain of the single mother still in high school and the middle-aged man newly paroled seeking employment. Yes, suffering is all around us—in us, our families, our loved ones, our churches, our communities, our cities, our nation, our world.

To respond with anything less than sincerity and authentic compassion would be a disservice to them and disrespect the devastation of their battles. When someone comes to me to share a burden, I always try to discern what they need from our time together. Sometimes they are seeking the wisdom of God's Word as they struggle with how to carry the weight of their present crisis. Others request prayer so that they know their hearts' cries are being heard by their pastor as well as their Good Shepherd.

And some people simply want their pain validated. They want to be heard and seen in the midst of what they're going through. They simply want to be reminded of the agape love of God transmitted through the sacrifice and suffering of His Son, Jesus Christ. For when we connect our suffering with the suffering of Jesus, we begin to glimpse how God redeems our pain for His purposes. Our pain is never wasted when we allow God to use it. In fact, our suffering makes us better lovers.

Lazy love refuses to suffer or sacrifice.

Lazy love only wants to take.

Lazy love refuses to address the pain.

Agape love suffers to save.

Agape love suffers to serve.

Agape love suffers to soothe.

At our church we use AGAPE as an acronym for the way our servant leaders shepherd our flock. An AGAPE leader serves with

Accountability and Guides with Authority to Protect our brand and Execute our vision. Our ministry, and I believe everyone's ministry both personal and pastoral, relies on agape love—the ability to feel compassion and to experience empathy with the suffering of others. This is the kind of agape love we see modeled by our Father's sacrificial gift—the life, death, and resurrection of His Son, Jesus Christ.

DISMANTLING OUR DEFENSES

Agape love—the supernatural, unmerited, gracious, generous love of our perfect Father—remains the basis for all other kinds of love. Agape love also serves as the most potent antidote to lazy love. Because as we experience more and more of God's lavish love and delight in us as His sons and daughters, we overflow with this divine love into all our relationships. Simply put, we receive the vertical love in order to experience the horizontal, thereby reflecting the cross and Christ's sacrifice for us.

Learning to experience God as our Abba Father is foundational to our faith and our ability to love. It is paramount to loving generously and without demanding or expecting anything in return. As we explored in the previous chapter, our relationships with our earthly fathers often stand in the way of experiencing God this way. Self-awareness goes a long way but only in revealing essential areas of forgiveness. So much of receiving our heavenly Daddy's lavish love is about dismantling our defenses and protective postures.

Many of those defenses and postures evolved from the way we reacted to pain in our lives. You'll recall that our attachment styles form very early as we adjust our expectations and behaviors based on what our parents and caregivers offer us—or are unable to provide for us. If we did not receive what we needed as infants, toddlers, and children, then we developed coping styles to try to get what we needed with as little pain as possible. The only problem is that these defensive systems carry over into adulthood when they are no longer needed and, in fact, become an intrusive obstacle to giving and receiving the kind of love we were made to enjoy and express.

Rather than working by default to avoid the pain, loss, and disappointments spilling over from our childhoods, we must learn to mature—both as adults and as believers—in order to grow closer to God and in our capacity to love others as He loves us. This is easier said than done, of course. But that's why it's so essential to experience the powerful agape love of Jesus. He knows all there is to know about human suffering, and that includes how to die to self and be resurrected to new life! Through Christ we find the power to experience healing and love others with the supernatural love of agape.

We can experience wholeness, no longer expecting others to provide something only Jesus can give us.

I DIDN'T SEE IT COMING

Long before Jesus suffered, died, and conquered death once and for all, God had sown seeds of hope through the message of His prophets. He used them to remind His people that He had not abandoned them. Due to their own rebellious choices, they distanced themselves from their Creator and Liberator, the One who had delivered them from the shackles of bondage in Egypt. The Israelites did not want to experience pain any more than you or I or any other human being. They wanted immediate gratification and instant deliverance from all their struggles. But God wanted more for them than comfort and convenience—He wanted them to grow up. And maturation always includes growing pains.

To reassure His people that He was with them always, God let them in on the bold, unimaginable plan already in motion: He was sending His only begotten Son, Jesus, the Word made flesh, to earth in human form. And the arrival of Jesus, the Messiah, the Immanuel of God with us, changed everything! So better than any movie trailer, preview of coming attractions, or teaser chapter of a book, the prophet Isaiah cast an unforgettable vision for the arrival of Christ and the impact it would have on humankind thereafter:

> The people walking in darkness
> > have seen a great light;
> on those living in the land of deep darkness
> > a light has dawned.
> You have enlarged the nation
> > and increased their joy;
> they rejoice before you
> > as people rejoice at the harvest,
> as warriors rejoice
> > when dividing the plunder...
>
> For to us a child is born,
> > to us a son is given,
> > and the government will be on his shoulders.
> And he will be called
> > Wonderful Counselor, Mighty God,
> > Everlasting Father, Prince of Peace.
> Of the greatness of his government and peace
> > there will be no end.
> He will reign on David's throne
> > and over his kingdom,
> establishing and upholding it

with justice and righteousness
from that time on and forever.
The zeal of the LORD Almighty
will accomplish this. (Isaiah 9:2–3, 6–7)

At the time Isaiah delivered God's message, the people of Israel probably struggled to imagine such an arrival—and perhaps many didn't care. The tribes of Israel had scattered, further fragmenting the faith of the people. Judah, as the Southern Kingdom was known, became famous for the way its people ignored God's commandments or went through the motions of offering sacrifices in the temple at Jerusalem. It was a lawless season of corruption and carnality as people rebelled against God's pursuit of their hearts.

God's people stubbornly refused to repent, and so the Lord allowed them to suffer the natural consequences of their sinful ways. In their striving they began to curse God and turn to the occult and pagan spiritualists and mediums: "Then they will look toward the earth and see only distress and darkness and fearful gloom, and they will be thrust into utter darkness" (Isa. 8:22).

Can you see the sharp contrast? Immediately on the heels of this pronounced observation, Isaiah's foretelling of the birth of Christ must have been radical and unimaginable. In the misery of their utter darkness, God sent them a candescent spark of radiant hope. The darkness would not endure because a great light would be dawning. There would be rejoicing in the kingdom again, the kind of celebrations held after winning a war. And the catalyst for this dramatic shift? A child being born, a Son being given, One whose reign would endure forever.

While it would take a few hundred years before the star blazed bright over a stable in Bethlehem, just the prospect of such a Messiah had to be thrilling. Did they dare to hope? Could order be restored? Would they live in the light again, with corruption conquered and justice prevailing? In the midst of their misery, hunger, and desperation, could they trust God to keep His promise?

You know the answer to these rhetorical questions, and yet I suspect you continue to ask them at times yourself. When the car breaks down and can't be fixed until payday. When your kids ditch school and you get a call from their teacher. When the doctor looks in your eyes with sadness to break the results of your biopsy. When your spouse's attorney serves you with divorce papers you never expected. When a yearlong relationship ends abruptly with a handful of words in a text. When your boss takes the credit for your work and gets promoted for it. When a parent or sibling dies unexpectedly. When we didn't see it coming.

We all have these "when" moments that cause us to pause and wonder if our faith is strong enough. If we dare to hope that even in these unbearable moments God is still with us. That He can meet us in our suffering and provide comfort, peace, healing, and whatever else is needed to rest in Him and move forward.

And the way God meets us in our suffering is through His Son.

LEAVE THE SHALLOWS BEHIND

In order to leave the shallows of lazy love behind and swim into the depths of God's agape love, we must accept the fullness of who God is as the Trinity, three persons in One—Father, Son, and Holy Spirit. Each person in the Godhead provides a unique aspect of love to us as God's children. We see each of the three reflected in Paul's benedictory blessing to the church at Corinth: "May the grace of the Lord Jesus Christ, and the love of God, and the fellowship of the Holy Spirit be with you all" (2 Cor. 13:14). We explored the Father-heart of God in our previous chapter, and we will shift into the power of the Holy Spirit in the next chapter. So let's consider what it means to receive God's love through, as Paul points out here, the grace of His Son, Jesus.

I have to believe Paul is quite intentional in the way he orders each member and their role in the Trinity here. It's surely no coincidence that the grace of the Lord Jesus Christ is mentioned first. Foremost, Jesus serves as the Intercessor, the Mediator, between us and God, between earth and heaven. You're probably aware that when we pray we do so in Jesus' name. Why? Because Jesus provides us access to His Father, who is our Father, too. Through Jesus we have relationship with the Holy and Almighty God. As I understand it, theologically we do not pray *to* Jesus but *through* Him because of His intercession on our behalf.

As the only member of the Trinity who lived on earth in human form, Jesus is uniquely qualified to know just how painful life can be. While fully God, Jesus was also fully human and hurt, cried, and felt pain like all human beings do. He also experienced the fullness of our emotions and the way we think and process our interactions with people and events in our lives. Our Lord and Savior knows exactly what we're going through! "For we do not have a high priest who is unable to empathize with our weaknesses, but we have one who has been tempted in every way, just as we are—yet he did not sin. Let us then approach God's throne of grace with confidence, so that we may receive mercy and find grace to help us in our time of need" (Heb. 4:15–16).

And yet He never sinned, which made His sacrifice holy and perfect, taking our place and paying the debt we could never afford. Not even with no down payment, 0 percent financing, and twenty-four months before the first payment comes due! No, we needed the sacrifice, and therefore the suffering, that only Jesus could provide. Now that we have access to the benefits of His sacrificial death and resurrection, we can receive mercy and find grace in our time of need. While it's available at any time and all the time, we're reminded here to be sure to receive it in our time of need—when we, too, are tempted, hurting, and suffering.

Yes, Jesus was tempted in every way possible that you and I or any other person has ever faced. He knew the full spectrum of all the human colors of thought, feeling, and desire. Other translations reflect these hues in ways that resonate so powerfully: The American Standard Version (ASV) tells us that Jesus knows what it's liked to be "touched with the feeling of our infirmities" (Heb. 4:15). In *The Message*, Eugene Peterson presents the truth of Jesus' dual identity—man and God—this way: "We don't have a priest who is out of touch with our reality. He's been through weakness and testing, experienced it all—all but the sin. So let's walk right up to him and get what he is so ready to give. Take the mercy, accept the help" (Heb. 4:15–16).

Did you hear that? Read that last sentence again, my friend!

Take the mercy, accept the help.

Take the mercy.

Accept the help.

SEPARATION IS IMPOSSIBLE

Without identification and acceptance of God as revealed in His Son, Jesus, you will get caught up in a performance trap—or even quit trying altogether. You may understand your need for a Savior theologically, but you are unwilling to surrender emotionally and psychologically. You appreciate the sonship of Jesus and His role in your salvation, but you don't own this relational awareness deep down in your being. Which means you must try harder to be a better person, to believe you are really forgiven, to overcome the guilt and shame of your failures and transgressions.

At some point, however, you will experience overwhelming spiritual exhaustion and likely withdraw and quit trying to know God and to please Him. Since you cannot do for yourself what Jesus came to do and has done for you, then you withhold yourself from communication with God. You backslide into old habits, default temptations, and familiar yet destructive ways of coping with your pain, failures, losses, fears, anxieties, and uncertainties.

Next time you're hurting, frightened, tempted, or in need, stop and tell Jesus what you need. Trust Him to take your needs instantly to God the Father and explain your situation. Look for the mercy that you can already access. Accept the help that the Lord provides!

Paul may have listed Jesus first in his benediction for another reason as well. Christ enables us to relate to God as coheirs, sons and daughters of our King, our heavenly Father. Without the grace received through Jesus, we could not approach God and maintain a personal relationship—our sin would get in the way.

Before Jesus became our perfect sacrifice, people would go to the tabernacle and make an animal sacrifice on the brazen altar, providing temporary cleansing so that they could proceed into the temple and encounter the holiness of God. Once Jesus died on the cross, though, His sacrifice cleansed us permanently and provided eternal access to God's presence.

On the cross Jesus paid our debt and gave us relational access to the Father, Son, and Holy Spirit. Jesus serves as our Intercessor and our Mediator, but He is also our beloved Savior, sacrificing Himself willingly, suffering unto death—and that basically means tortured to death—on our behalf. He turned the cross into our bridge from earth to heaven. He conquered sin and death so that we might know God and live victoriously as we fulfill our divine purpose and advance God's kingdom. We receive the gift of grace through the suffering and sacrifice of Jesus, and by grace we are saved (see Eph. 2:8–9). Because of His grace, nothing can separate us from the love of God!

> "For I am convinced that neither death nor life, neither angels nor demons, neither the present nor the future, nor any powers, neither height nor depth, nor anything else in all creation, will be able to separate us from the love of God that is in Christ Jesus our Lord." (Romans 8:38–39)

Separation from God's love is impossible because of what Jesus has done for us!

Knowing you can never be separated from the eternal wellspring of Love's fountain, you can give others the living water for which they thirst—without ever diminishing your own supply.

LOVE ANYTHING

If there is literally nothing—no thing—that can separate us from the love of God because of the grace we have in Jesus, then we are forced to rethink how we handle pain. Rather than reinforce our defenses and broken attachment styles, rather than trying to escape and numb our pain, what if we dared to surrender our suffering to the One who suffered most on our behalf?

When calamitous circumstances cause us to pause, when a personal crisis sends us crashing to the floor of our limitations, then we are forced to choose how we suffer. We can run away from it, resist it, ignore it, repress it, or become a victim in it. Or we can run toward the suffering, embrace it, acknowledge it, express it, and become more than a conqueror through our faith in Jesus Christ.

If you want to love more fully and completely, then your choice is clear: "To love at all is to be vulnerable," wrote iconic writer, theologian, and apologist C. S. Lewis:

> Love anything and your heart will be wrung and possibly broken. If you want to make sure of keeping it intact you must give it to no one, not even an animal. Wrap it carefully round with hobbies and little luxuries; avoid all entanglements. Lock it up safe in the casket or coffin of your selfishness. But in that casket, safe, dark, motionless, airless, it will change. It will not be broken; it will become unbreakable, impenetrable, irredeemable. To love is to be vulnerable.[1]

If we agree with Lewis that to love is to be vulnerable, then we must risk being open, honest, and authentic. We must not pretend that there is nothing at stake or that we are not risking the likelihood of future pain. Love requires that we exercise our strength by relying on God's power, enabling us to love far beyond our human abilities. When we suffer, we tend to become self-absorbed and blinded to the pain and needs of others. Lazy love settles for selfish love, but God's agape love always endures more, gives more, carries more.

When we attempt to avoid suffering, our love grows lazy and stagnates. We cut ourselves off from the Source, who can help us love beyond ourselves. At best, we love within our human capacity and capabilities—which we know are limited, finite, subjective, and moody. Attempting to love while avoiding suffering is akin to attempting to swim while avoiding deep water. You can still splash around in puddles and wading pools, but you cannot immerse yourself and glide with a current greater than yourself through the depths.

In his timeless reflection on love in 1 Corinthians 13, Paul assures us that love "endures all things" and "never fails" (vv. 7–8 NKJV). Agape love bears the unbearable and never fails to show up and make God's love known. The price of love is ultimately suffering—but the cost of God's grace through Jesus is priceless. We disconnect our default human tendency for lazy love when we recognize the gift of grace we've been given.

LOVE ANYWAY

Allowing God to transform our suffering into a sacrifice that serves and soothes others requires surrender. It requires a willingness to love despite the pain, the loss, the ache, and the hurt we carry inside from our past mistakes and the wounds of others. Rather than refusing to look beyond our own suffering and offer what we can to others, through the agape love of Jesus we find the strength, the power, and the stamina to give despite our own deficits. We acknowledge that we have not been loved the way we were made to be loved. And we accept that these wounds have affected our own capacity to love others.

Notice the difference, too, between acknowledging and accepting our wounding. Acknowledging simply means recognizing the fact that we failed to get the love we needed. Our acknowledgment looks into the truth and refuses to flinch. We refuse to ignore, refute, or deny that what happened actually happened. Yes, our father abandoned us. Yes, our mother ignored us and favored our younger sibling. Yes, our teacher harmed us. Yes, someone betrayed our trust and used us, abused us, and shamed us into silence. Acknowledgment is the starting line for healing, for moving into acceptance.

Acceptance is required in order to move forward and to receive the healing God offers us. When we accept our wounds and the losses of love we've endured, we can then grieve them properly and cry out to God for His peace, His presence, and His power in those wounds. This kind of surrender cannot happen merely by acknowledging what we've lost and suffered. Acceptance takes our pain and weaves it into our story without making it the central thread of our story. Acceptance allows us to carry it without being weighed down by its burden. And the only way this can happen is supernaturally.

When we're willing to look at how we've been wounded and the consequences, we can then begin to see how we have failed to love others. We can do better than we've done before. We can suffer and tell the truth and choose to love anyway. We can refuse to let the enemy have the last laugh or the final word and instead choose to live in the selfless love and resurrection power of the living Christ. We can move through our devastation, disappointments, and destruction and allow God to use them as bridges to the hearts of others in their suffering.

If you want to overcome lazy love, then going through this door is not an option. You may love others well enough and make some small strides. You may be willing to stay in your marriage and to tolerate the antics of others. You might even feel good about yourself as a Christian because you're willing to serve in your church, your neighborhood, and your community. But until you deal with the issue of your own suffering, you will always hit a wall. You will almost always feel justified at giving love with limits.

And giving love with limits, well, that's just lazy love.

Limitless love is possible only when you rely on a supernatural source of love for the power required to endure all things, bear all things, and not be destroyed by them. Others wanted to harm you, to belittle you, to shame you, to use you, to kill you—but somehow you have survived and now God is using what was done to you for His precious purposes. Your pain is not wasted but transformed.

And the secret to this transformation?

The third facet of God's love as supplied by the Holy Spirit!

In our exploration of agape love, we've reconsidered what it means to know and love God as our perfect Father in heaven. We've just explored how we can be loved and love others more powerfully through the grace of Jesus. So now it's time to consider how agape is fueled—by the power of the Holy Spirit!

CHAPTER 6

The Spirit of Agape Love

To love someone means to see him as God intended him.
                                        —Fyodor Dostoyevsky

I love team sports and my favorite has always been basketball. Back in college I had the privilege of playing on our school's team and experienced the thrill of being part of something that needed my contribution while also multiplying my efforts because of the shared commitment of my teammates. This awareness of our connection proved to be a critical motivator when I tore my ACL not once but *twice* within a five-month period. Rather than allow these injuries to impede my passion for the game, I concentrated on how much the team needed me—and how much I needed them.

Rehab was brutally hard and slammed me against the limits of my pain threshold every day. I hated each minute of the physical therapy and painful exercises I endured during my recovery. But I loved the game—and that thrill of being part of something bigger than my individual talent—enough to push through the pain. And when I returned, I went on to have the highest point, rebound, and assist averages of my career!

SWEET HARMONY

As part of that team, I especially loved our synchronicity on the court when we functioned with one mind, one heart, one strategy. This harmony would manifest when another player threw the ball my way, knowing exactly where I would be and how I would already be anticipating taking my shot. While part of our connection relied on knowing the plays and postures called by our coaches, the best games reflected our interdependence on one another. Timing was indeed everything! We knew one another's strengths and weaknesses as well as abilities and limitations, and we maximized them to work together.

I have also experienced this kind of cohesive collaboration of talent when making music. It's no secret that music, whether a stadium concert by a solo performer or a multiperson praise and worship band in an intimate church setting, relies on cooperative collaboration. Each musician playing an instrument knows their part, when to come in and when to hold back, and how to blend beautifully to accompany the human voices interweaving their audial input. Technicians, sound engineers, and producers also play vital roles to bring all the sounds together for the desired impact shared by all involved—a sweet harmony greater than the sum of its parts.

You won't be surprised to learn that I have also been part of teams and music groups that lacked this kind of collaborative cohesion. In sports, I've encountered the egos of many would-be superstars, talented players intent on showboating their way to success, with or without the team. Some teams, though, don't come together even when there is humility and superb talent; for whatever reason the unifying factor elevating everyone's ability is missing.

In music, I've similarly experienced participants who wanted to outshine the lead singer rather than contribute the requested backup vocals. Or sometimes it might be a group of talented musicians who simply do not jell despite their tremendous individual talents. The ingredients are there, but the glue of being in sync remains absent. Somehow the collection of separate persons fails to unify. They miss each other's abilities, overlook opportunities, and seem oblivious to the potential of their team as a whole.

What makes the difference between a synchronized team or harmonious group and the ones that stumble off-key? And what does this have to do with agape love? I can't wait to tell you!

Because it's the secret to overcoming this major threat to your relationships—withholding your heart.

PERFECT ATTUNEMENT

Many qualities work to create successful teams: preparation, training, leadership, communication, and shared vision, just to name a few. The ability to work in harmony with others, however, seems to rely on a kind of bond among group members. Psychologists often call this quality *attunement*—a term that extends far beyond championship teams and award-winning albums to encompass virtually all human relationships. Scholar and psychotherapist Odelya Kraybill defines attunement as "a nonverbal process of being with another person in a way that attends fully and responsively to that person. Attunement is interactive and provided with supportive eye contact, vocalization, speech, and body language."[1]

Psychologically speaking, emotional attunement describes the way parents respond to their children, anticipating their needs, responding to their cries, and providing security through their presence. Attuned parents are literally tuned in to the age, stage, and page their kids are on at any given time. When a mother is attuned, she hears her infant crying in the church nursery in a way distinct from all the other babies. When a father is attuned, he senses his daughter's anxiety on the first day of school and walks her into her classroom.

But attunement has now become a buzzword for the way people connect in other various roles and contexts. When a husband anticipates the exhaustion of his overextended wife and prepares her favorite comfort food, he is attuned to her. When a wife knows the love language of her husband and selects the perfect gift for his birthday, she is attuned to him. When a supervisor picks up on the exhaustion of her team members and knows they need a break before continuing, she's using attunement. When a coach instinctively understands which players are emotionally prepared to play their best game, he's attuned to both individuals along with the team as a whole.

Attunement requires observing, listening, and paying close attention. As two people begin dating and getting to know each other, their bond grows as they see each other fully and understand one another in ways that seem intuitive or even instinctive. They listen and observe with their senses as well as their hearts and notice details, expressions, body language, and what is said as well as what goes unsaid. They notice patterns and begin to anticipate the other person's needs and responses while allowing room for spontaneity and the unexpected.

IN THE KEY OF LOVE

As you can imagine, attunement extends to the awareness between teachers and pupils, coaches and players, supervisors and employees. The best, most effective and successful leaders may appear to have a natural gift for attunement to those around them. They listen carefully, communicate frequently, and provide numerous opportunities for their followers to take risks, to learn from failures, and to persevere in problem-solving. Whether it comes naturally to them or not, these leaders value the power of emotional and psychological alignment to accomplish team goals and motivate excellence, and therefore productivity. Leaders of this caliber both demonstrate and orchestrate harmony in the key of love.

They model servant leadership and embody the example Jesus set for His followers when washing their feet at their final meal together before the Crucifixion. When Peter objected that he could never allow his Master, the Messiah, to perform such a humble task, Jesus explained: "Very truly I tell you, no servant is greater than his master, nor is a messenger greater than the one who sent him. Now that you know these things, you will be blessed if you do them" (John 13:16–17).

Considering the role attunement plays in effective relationships, how have you experienced attunement in your own life? Who is in your life right now that often seems attuned to your moods, needs, and expectations? Who is in your life right now that you feel attuned to?

Not surprisingly, *lazy love thrives when there is lack of attunement.* Without attunement, your heart begins to wither and atrophy.

When we fail to attune to others, or sense others are not attuned to us, we tend to become more self-reliant, defensive, and independent. We feel entitled and want others to wash our feet and wait on us because of our importance, title, role, or authority. Without attuning to the moods and needs of those around us, we turn our gaze inward and grow lazy in loving beyond ourselves.

While some people have a gift for compassion and empathy, sensing and absorbing the emotions around them and registering an overall vibe, others are almost exclusively focused on themselves.

They barely notice the people in their lives, even the ones supposedly closest, like spouses, kids, coworkers, and neighbors. They rarely listen but instead offer a running monologue focused on their lives, their needs, and their ongoing expectations. They take more than they give and often aren't bothered by this pattern in their lives. They focus on social media as a barometer for their self-worth and success.

While self-absorbed people may lack attunement and default to lazy love, every human being shares the tendency to focus on themselves more than others. Depending on our attachment styles, and what we did and didn't receive while growing up, from others who may or may not have been attuned to us, we all struggle to varying degrees at times. We want to love our neighbors as ourselves, but we're also committed to avoiding pain and acquiring pleasure. We want to lead by serving, but we also want the power and the respect that come with authority. We want to offer compassion and kindness to everyone around us, but we also wait to see how others treat us first.

Fortunately, we're not limited by our own human tendencies and past emotional deficits. As we've already noted, the unconditional and supernatural agape love of God allows us to love beyond ourselves. When we experience God as our perfect and loving Father, we're no longer looking to others to fill the hole inside our hearts that only God can fill. When we encounter the sacrificial suffering of Jesus, the Son of God, we want others to experience the same grace and mercy that transformed our lives. And when the Holy Spirit of God indwells us, we have the power to love others in ways that transcend our human limits and selfish interests.

With the Holy Spirit in our lives, we can extend agape love in perfect attunement.

DIVINE LOVE GENERATOR

Of the three persons of the Trinity, the Holy Spirit seems the hardest to grasp, at least for many people. Perhaps it's the role and how this aspect of God is named, but the Holy Spirit, also known as the Holy Ghost, may seem more mysterious and inscrutable than the Father and the Son. At least on earth we know about fathers and sons, but the concept of the Spirit usually tilts people toward the charismatic or toward the spooky. Either the Holy Spirit is viewed as the essence of God that descends on us as a catalyst for irrational behavior—such as speaking in unknown spiritual languages or laughing uncontrollably in holy mirth—or as an unpredictable entity that frightens more than fortifies.

While there is a semblance of truth in those extreme perspectives, the actuality of the Holy Spirit is more intimate, loving, and empowering than you may realize. Keep in mind that the Spirit is a gift that God sent His children on earth after Jesus had risen from the grave and ascended into heaven. Even before His departure, Christ tried to prepare His followers for this supernatural gift:

> All this I have spoken while still with you. But the Advocate, the Holy Spirit, whom the Father will send in my name, will teach you all things and will remind you of everything I have said to you. Peace I leave with you; my peace I give you. I do not give to you as the world gives. Do not let your hearts be troubled and do not be afraid. (John 14:25–27)

Notice that Jesus' description doesn't describe the Holy Spirit as overpowering or frightening. Instead, Christ concisely describes the Spirit's role—that of Advocate, teacher, reminder, truth-teller, peace-giver, and Comforter. The Greek word that is usually translated as

Holy Spirit is *parakletos*, which literally means "one called to be by one's side." We have nothing to fear and everything to gain when we experience God's presence through His Spirit living in us. He is the gift we receive when we accept the free gift of God's grace and choose to follow Christ.

While we pray to our Father and pray to and in Jesus' name as our Intercessor, the Holy Spirit is the person of the Trinity who lives with us as we encounter our daily ups and downs. He is our ultimate BFF, the divine friend sent from heaven to be with us here on earth. The Spirit is our Advocate, guardian, champion, and a uniquely distinct Intercessor who acts in addition to the intercession that Jesus provides.

The Spirit empowers us with God's strength in the midst of our weakness and intercedes on our behalf when we don't even know what we need—now that is a friend indeed! In his letter to the Romans, Paul explains, "In the same way, the Spirit helps us in our weakness. We do not know what we ought to pray for, but the Spirit himself intercedes for us through wordless groans. And he who searches our hearts knows the mind of the Spirit, because the Spirit intercedes for God's people in accordance with the will of God" (Rom. 8:26–27). This spiritual power includes the strength needed to resist temptation. We are unable to resist in our own power so God gives us a direct, divine connection to His limitless power.

Yes, we may still experience internal conflict at times and even yield to temptation and fail to obey God. In the same epistle, Paul expressed this frustration experienced at various times by every follower of Christ: "I do not understand what I do. For what I want to do I do not do, but what I hate I do" (Rom. 7:15). The good news of the Spirit in us, however, eclipses our failures and empowers us to persevere, maintaining our connection to God and prompting us to repent and turn our attention and direction back toward the example set by Christ. Paul refers to this as having our "minds set on what the Spirit desires" rather than the sinful inclinations of "what the flesh desires" (Rom. 8:5). Once the Spirit of God lives in you, you "are not in the realm of the flesh but are in the realm of the Spirit" (Rom. 8:9).

Through the power of the Spirit in us, we can find reserves of patience, compassion, kindness, and service that transcend our human capacities. This ability reflects what the Bible calls the fruit of the Spirit—"love, joy, peace, forbearance, kindness, goodness, faithfulness, gentleness and self-control" (Gal. 5:22–23). The divine fruit of the Spirit in you enables you to respond with patience and self-control when you're tired and grumpy and want to snap at your kids. You serve up the spiritual fruit in you when you exercise self-control and refuse to respond to your coworker's desire to flirt and gossip. Spiritual fruit in you allows you to see beyond the rude demeanor of your waitress and attune to the challenging day she must be having.

Some of these qualities can obviously be conditioned into us through our parents, our peers, socialization, and cultural etiquette. But such conditioning still hits the wall of human limitations sooner or later. It is only through our power in the Spirit that we can love others the way Jesus loves them. The Holy Spirit is our divine love generator—kicking in when our human capacity to love short-circuits.

LOVING JUDAS

Stuck in traffic recently, I saw a bumper sticker on the vehicle in front of me that nailed it: "The test of Christianity is not loving Jesus—it's loving Judas." Loving, forgiving, and showing compassion to the people who betray us, harm us, injure us, ignore us, demean us, and wound us is never easy. And I would venture basically impossible if not for the agape love of God demonstrated through the love of His Son and poured into us through the love of His Spirit. Left to our own reactions and responses, most people become consumed by hatred, rage, revenge, and retaliation against those who have offended them. Sometimes we feel this impulse when someone cuts us off on the highway or leaves a nasty comment on our latest post online. When the stakes and the impact of the injury are so much greater, then that desire gets exponentially multiplied.

This human tendency to react and retaliate reveals another way the Holy Spirit enables us to transform the agape love, grace, and mercy we have experienced from God into the ability to forgive those whose cuts run deepest in our souls. Jesus instructed us to pray, "Forgive us our sins, as we have forgiven those who sin against us" (Matt. 6:12 NLT). And based on other comments Jesus made, it's clear that forgiveness requires more than going through the motions or making a onetime choice.

Peter once asked Jesus how many times it was necessary to forgive someone who had sinned against him, wondering if it required as many as seven times, as indicated by Jewish law for the worst offenses. Christ answered by blowing up any legalistic attempt to forgive a set number of times: "I tell you, not seven times, but seventy-seven times" (Matt. 18:22). To drive home his point, Jesus then shared a parable:

> Therefore, the kingdom of heaven is like a king who wanted to settle accounts with his servants. As he began the settlement, a man who owed him ten thousand bags of gold was brought to him. Since he was not able to pay, the master

ordered that he and his wife and his children and all that he had be sold to repay the debt.

At this the servant fell on his knees before him. "Be patient with me," he begged, "and I will pay back everything." The servant's master took pity on him, canceled the debt and let him go.

But when that servant went out, he found one of his fellow servants who owed him a hundred silver coins. He grabbed him and began to choke him. "Pay back what you owe me!" he demanded.

His fellow servant fell to his knees and begged him, "Be patient with me, and I will pay it back."

But he refused. Instead, he went off and had the man thrown into prison until he could pay the debt. When the other servants saw what had happened, they were outraged and went and told their master everything that had happened.

Then the master called the servant in. "You wicked servant," he said, "I canceled all that debt of yours because you begged me to. Shouldn't you have had mercy on your fellow servant just as I had on you?" In anger his master handed him over to the jailers to be tortured, until he should pay back all he owed.

This is how my heavenly Father will treat each of you unless you forgive your brother or sister from your heart. (Matthew 18:23–35)

Jesus emphasized that we must focus on our own shortcomings and sinful offenses against others rather than becoming a victim to the ways others hurt us. It's not that we must ignore our wounds or pretend that others have not sinned against us; it's that we must not use these injuries to become blind to our own sinful tendencies.

We must remain humble and fully aware of the grace we have been given in order to extend this same mercy and loving-kindness to others. Jesus rebuked hypocrites refusing to acknowledge their own brokenness and focusing instead on the faults of others: "Why do you look at the speck of sawdust in your brother's eye and pay no attention to the plank in your own eye?" (Matt. 7:3). Just as we do not deserve God's grace and cannot earn it, overcoming lazy love mandates that we must extend the same power of forgiveness to those who sin against us.

God's Spirit in you provides the fuel for this kind of forgiveness. The Spirit reminds you of God's agape love for you even when you stumble, struggle, and fall—and also reminds you to offer the same kind of supernatural love to others when they do the same. Forgiveness fueled by agape love does not forget the offenses and does not ignore the consequences or the impact of others' sinful actions. But forgiveness fueled by agape love does refuse to harbor bitterness that festers into resentment and poisons your soul.

CONQUERING LAZY LOVE

If you want to love boldly and bravely, then you need a constant connection to the lavish, unconditional, unmerited, delight-in-you love of God. This connection comes through the Holy Spirit living in you, which in turn allows you to become a conduit of this same agape love. Cultivating your relationship with the Holy Spirit allows you to experience more of God's agape love. A richer, deeper experience of divine agape love transforms your ability to love others—especially those who are not easy to love.

Cultivation requires communication by praying and opening your heart to God's Spirit dwelling in you. This is not something mysterious or formal and there is not one proper way to do it. Simply think about how you relate and talk to your closest friends. Think of growing closer to the Spirit as building a deep friendship with someone who knows you better than you know yourself—and still loves you. As you grow in intimacy with this person of God, you naturally overflow with agape love for those around you. This allows you to attune to people who are difficult, overly needy, selfish, angry, hurting, and wounded.

Rather than avoiding your coworker who always brags about their latest amazing vacation, when empowered by God's Spirit you're able to love this person. To see through her insecurities and unspoken desire to be seen, loved, and accepted. Rather than reacting in anger to your child's misbehavior, the Spirit-led parent experiences the strength to exercise patience, compassion, and wisdom. To view their son or daughter in a greater context of grace, the same grace they themselves have experienced directly from God.

Instead of retaliating when your spouse hurts your feelings, you can communicate openly and honestly and discuss what occurred, resisting the temptation to withdraw, pout, and hurt them in similar ways. Instead of being too busy to help your elderly neighbor with her yard work, you offer before she asks and promptly get it done. Instead of mentally checking out when your close friend complains yet again about her marriage, you remain engaged and fully present, listening closely without trying to solve her problems, simply holding space with her during a challenging season.

When we experience God's Spirit living in us, we have the ability to overcome lazy love by loving those—including ourselves—who sometimes seem unlovable. Yes, how we love often varies from person to person and context to context. In other words, love looks different depending on the dynamics of your particular relationship. Living and loving in God's Spirit is a great equalizer, however. There is no one you cannot love—even abusers, traitors, betrayers, liars, cheaters, thieves, and assassins of your character and reputation—with God's Spirit pouring agape love into your heart. I do not say this lightly because I know how unimaginable it seems to forgive others for the horrendous, heinous, sometimes evil ways they wound us.

But believing that you are justified in refusing to love and forgive anyone else is refusing agape and choosing lazy love instead. When your heart is breaking, lazy love takes the easy route and often avoids conflict, confrontation, and challenges. Lazy love holds evidence against others and feels entitled to manipulate and take more than it gives.

Lazy love wants to skate on the surface and focus on self-interests more than on loving others. But it's not loving to continue enabling someone who's wrestling an addiction, even if refusing to might cause a rupture in your friendship. Nor is it loving to pretend like nothing happened when you're actually seething inside because you feel exploited by your boss. Lazy love cheats others when they don't love you the way you want or feel entitled to be loved.

Lazy love also cheats you. Without ongoing relationship with God through His Spirit within you, your growth will be stalled, stunted, and stuck in place. You will likely have established a basic foundational connection to God and with Jesus, but in the face of life's overwhelming demands and disruptions, you are limited by self-reliance and self-sufficiency. Agape love empowers you to do what you cannot do on your own.

Without friendship with the Holy Spirit, you limit your ability to grow, to change, to transform, and to love more effectively. You need divine agape love as your power source; otherwise, you will continue to limit your capacity to love based on human understanding, emotional fluctuations, and self-directed fulfillment. We can love our neighbors as ourselves only when we have experienced the satisfying and sustaining love of God.

When the Spirit of God dwells in you, however, you are more than a conqueror over lazy love. Through the power of the Spirit, your love laser-focuses the supernatural agape of God, the kind of love that is irrational, illogical, and unstoppable. Fueled by the Spirit, you are naturally attuned to and can give yourself wholeheartedly to everyone around you. As you grow closer to God and more intimate with His Spirit, lazy love transforms into crazy love. You can give away your love fearlessly and joyfully!

Experiencing the fullness of the Trinity through agape love overcomes the threat of withholding yourself and settling for lazy love—every time.

THREAT #2

Posturing Defensively due to Lack of Phileo

Love must be sincere. Hate what is evil; cling to what is good. Be devoted to one another in love. Honor one another above yourselves. Never be lacking in zeal, but keep your spiritual fervor, serving the Lord. Be joyful in hope, patient in affliction, faithful in prayer. Share with the Lord's people who are in need. Practice hospitality.

ROMANS 12:9-13

The overriding character trait of Jesus is love, and the entire Gospel story is woven with love. Sometimes it's not easy, and oftentimes it requires sacrifice, but it's when we love that we are the most like Jesus.

STEVEN FURTICK

CHAPTER 7

Companions and Confidants

Lots of people want to ride with you in the limo, but what you want is someone who will take the bus with you when the limo breaks down.

—Oprah Winfrey

In a secluded city park just below Nashville's 12 South district, two friends, both professional musicians in Music City, meet for a weekly high five. Depending on the weather, temperature, and time of year, sometimes they chat for a few minutes and shoot baskets on a nearby court. Other weeks, they find a bench in the shade or sit beneath the canopy of a mature elm tree and catch up on anything and everything. When they're both busy and covered up with work, they meet, snap their fingers, and do a silent high five, nod, and then retrace their steps for almost a mile in opposite directions to their respective homes.

Andy Gullahorn and Gabe Scott have been friends for more than two decades and have been meeting to high-five for about half that time. When Gabe battled encephalitis, the swelling in his brain caused most of his memories to disappear. Andy was there in the hospital with him as much as possible, and once Gabe started recovery, one day Andy asked him for a high five. The simple act triggered Gabe's memory of the many times they had walked in all kinds of weather to see each other.[1]

Over time, Gabe has since recovered many of his memories. Their story of friendship has been featured in numerous media sources, including *CBS Sunday Morning* and the *Atlantic*. He and Andy continue their tradition, and Andy even wrote a song, "Small Things," about the powerful connection emerging from such a seemingly trivial, even silly, action.

You may have your own small things—little rituals, inside jokes, catchphrases, and secret signals—with someone you consider a close or best friend. In fact, I hope you do. Because the sad reality is that for all the talk about online friendships and social media community, millions of people suffer from a relational deficit that is harming their physical and mental health. Even while writing this chapter, I saw the US surgeon general, Vivek Murthy, hold a press conference to announce his department's "National Strategy to Advance Social Connection" to help overcome our nation's "epidemic of loneliness and isolation."

According to Dr. Murthy, even prior to the COVID-19 pandemic that started in 2020, approximately half of all adults in our country—roughly 150 million people—experienced loneliness on a regular and consistent basis. The quarantines, isolation, and precautions to prevent the spread of the pandemic created a greater gap between individuals and their families, friends, neighbors, and support systems.[2]

Dr. Murthy cited the catalog of illnesses, diseases, and health challenges caused in part and compounded by isolation and loneliness, including insomnia, depression, anxiety, and chronic pain. "In people of all ages, they may be associated with higher risks of heart disease, stroke, diabetes, addiction, suicidality and self-harm, and dementia." The primary solution comes down to social connections that form a scaffold of community that supports and facilitates deeper, richer friendships. Murthy asserted, "Social connection is as essential to humanity as food, water or shelter, the advisory says."[3]

This assertion is not simply a matter of medical opinion.

The emphasis on phileo love in God's Word makes it a matter of necessity.

DEEP AND WIDE

Think back over your life for a moment and make note of the friends who have made the greatest investments in who you are right now. Your season of friendship with them may have lasted days or even hours, and some will span decades from childhood until present day. If you immediately think you have too many to count, then narrow your focus to close friends, not acquaintances, colleagues, and associates. These friends saw you, got you, and loved you for who you are and allowed you to glimpse them authentically as well.

How many come to mind? A handful? A dozen? More? How did the duration of each friendship enrich your life? How did it enhance your friend's?

After considering the breadth of your friendships over the years, assess the depth of those friendships that came to mind. Who has walked with you through dark valleys and deep waters? Who related only at a surface level of pleasant camaraderie? Who kept it light and laid-back and who brought substance and intensity?

The most impactful, life-giving friendships tend to run deep and wide.

You've shared big events together—graduations, weddings, births of children, moves, career changes, divorces, funerals. But you've also enjoyed time just living life—talking about the ball game or your latest binge-fave series, going on walks or hiking together, shopping and enjoying meals together. You can laugh together and skate on the surface or deep-dive to search for the sunken treasure below.

Looking at both the horizontal and the vertical aspects of your friendships can be very telling about the kinds of friends you tend to gravitate toward. The quantity and quality of your friendships also provide a barometer of your physical, mental, and spiritual health. Perhaps you're blessed in your assessment with an extensive network of long-standing friendships that have consistently improved your life. Do not be alarmed, however, if your reflection left you sadly lacking the bonds and blessings others may take for granted.

Perhaps you find yourself having numerous friendships that reach a certain level of relationship but fail to go further, to establish a deeper, longer-lasting connection. Or you may tell yourself that you're simply too busy to invest in friendships at this current season of your life. It's possible that you've talked yourself into believing the enemy's lie that you don't need others, that they will always let you down, that friendships never return the precious personal resources invested. You may be tired of always being the one who initiates and sustains the relationships you have in hopes of experiencing the soul friends you long to know.

Whatever barriers to life-giving friendships you may have experienced, you are most definitely not alone. With the countless number of distractions, demands, and disruptions on our lives today, the deep phileo-type of friendship, the kind mentioned in the

Scriptures and the kind you long to enjoy, requires intentionality. It necessitates taking ownership of those small things that help keep you connected. And while texting, emails, and video chats are wonderful ways to sustain your friendship lifeline, they are no substitute for in-person face time, for shared experiences in real time, and for leisurely discussions without watching the clock.

While busyness and lack of time are the reasons we often cite for not enjoying richer friendships, the greatest threat lies within us. Without a grasp of phileo love, we often resort to posturing to become who or what we think our friends want or need us to be. We want their friendship desperately enough to compromise our authenticity. Rather than allow them to experience us honestly and vulnerably, we posture and pose, compare and compete.

This threat can be overcome—if you're willing to risk more by posturing less.

LAZY LOVE LIMITS

If you're not drawing from agape love as your source, it becomes challenging to love others as yourself. Instead, you likely get caught up in loving conditionally quid pro quo. Rather than giving and receiving phileo love with other people in rich, deeply connected friendships, you might become a pleaser or doormat, a manipulator or bully—or most likely a hybrid blend in between these extremes. Friendship becomes a matter of back-scratching—you provide something I need and I'll provide something you need—and results in volatility, instability, and convenience.

Without experiencing phileo love, you compare yourself to others and bounce between feeling less than them, which causes you to scramble and compensate, and feeling better than them, which inflates your prideful ego into arrogant isolation. Simply put, you posture, putting on masks and personae, costumes and roles, like a seasoned character actor who has become adept at playing the part required for that moment's performance. To be known authentically, you must drop the postures of performance.

I've learned the power of phileo love firsthand. If you ask me to reflect on the friendships that have had the greatest impact on me, I'm inclined to tell you about the friends who meet me where I am right now. A few of these are deep-rooted friendships I've maintained since my adolescence and college years, but most have only been planted recently but are already bearing fruit. Some of these friends might not surprise you, but I suspect many might pique your curiosity.

One of the greatest false assumptions, intuitive fallacies, and conditioned biases is that meaningful, lasting friendships can happen only with people like ourselves. I am an adult Black male, a husband and a father, called to full-time ministry and leadership in the body of Christ, and I have a few phileo-type friendships with other adult Black males who are married with children and serve in ministry. But to limit myself to deep relationships with only people who are the same age, generation, race, ethnicity, gender, education level, belief system, profession, denomination, and economic level creates a net that filters out countless individuals with whom I might experience exceptional relationships.

These kinds of limitations are rarely conscious choices but are—you guessed it—the result of lazy love. Why? Because lazy love hates to take risks. Risks require an investment without a guaranteed return; risks pull us out of our comfort zone and into uncertainty; risks challenge social and cultural norms. Lazy love settles instead for trying to please others in order to get ahead, to shun those who cannot advance our interests, and to assess others based on appearances. Lazy love plays it safe and reinforces comfort, security, and reputation.

If Jesus had succumbed to the human tendency of loving lazily, then He would likely have surrounded Himself with safe, political, easy choices—the movers and shakers of His day, the leaders and trendsetters, the influencers and affluent, Pharisees and Sadducees, the Jewish elite and not the mongrel masses. But we know Jesus exemplifies the essence of His Father's love in human form and demonstrates a love that is inclusive, compassionate, accepting, and selfless.

The people whom Jesus chose as His closest friends, His twelve disciples, were an assortment of misfits, misanthropes, and mavericks—working-class men who fished, a tax collector despised by the culture, and others who may have had no career path. The people whom Jesus chose to associate with were often considered to be social outcasts—prostitutes, adulterers, lepers, the impoverished, and non-Jewish immigrants. It appears Jesus extended His divine love to literally every human being—men, women, and children—He encountered.

When we resort to limiting, either deliberately or subconsciously, the kind of people who can be our friends, we miss out on extraordinary opportunities to learn more about ourselves, about what it means to be human, and about what it means to know God. Some of the most memorable and impactful friends are the ones who surprise you the most. The ones that you appear to have little or nothing in common with. Or the ones that have so much in common with you, it might seem like you're in competition.

My experience certainly reflects that God enjoys using diversity, unpredictability, and humility in our friendships to expand our hearts, deepen our faith, and stretch our minds.

COMPETE VS. COMPLETE

One of my life's greatest and longest-lasting friendships almost didn't happen. Not because we didn't have common interests, shared goals, and similar convictions but because we competed against one another. Brad and I were college roommates—and we were both intent on starting as the shooting guard on the basketball team, which meant we were immediately competitors.

Two competitors couldn't be more different. I was six-foot-four and Brad was five-foot-eleven on a good day with shoes on with thick soles. My vertical was measured at about forty-one inches. Brad's? Well, let's just say it was never measured. I once jumped over Brad in a dunk contest. All I am trying to do is explain the vast differences in our physical abilities. We were not similarly matched physically or athletically. But Brad had two distinct advantages, in my view, that worked in my friend's favor: his work ethic and the fact that his father happened to be the coach of the team.

I hoped that my occasional shift from disappointment to resentment went unnoticed, and to his credit, Brad remained humble, focused, and a generous team player. So generous, in fact, that when he started struggling and couldn't get out of a slump, he told our coach, his dad, that I should have his spot! His father agreed and I've never forgotten Brad's willingness to sacrifice his ego for my sake and the sake of our team.

Because that's what friendships forged by phileo love do. True friends make sacrifices. They introduce you to yourself and help you see who you really are. I didn't know I was good enough to play that position the way it needed to be played, the way our team deserved, until Brad told me.

We have remained friends for more than two decades now. Brad became one of the most successful real estate agents in Indiana and, of course, sold me my first house. We still talk on a regular basis and see each other when schedules permit, catching up on our families, our careers, our faith, and, depending on the time of year, how our favorite college and NBA teams are faring. We discuss the books we've been reading, share the struggles we're facing, and confide in the trust we've built over the past twenty years.

As we conclude a conversation, it's not unusual for Brad to ask me, "How can I serve you?" And after I answer him, I shoot the question back at him. Because our friendship endures on more than a foundation of shared experiences and our old glory days. Our friendship thrives because love always seeks to serve.

GIFTS OF THE WISE MEN

This hallmark emerges in a much more recent friendship with someone in a very different season of life than Brad or myself. I first met Roscoe Smith on the golf course not far from my house a few years ago. Since then I've learned that he's in his eighties, which means he's almost twice my age, and maintains a perspective that I can't help but envy. Roscoe has a gift for seeing life through the eyes of a lifelong golfer, one who has never stopped working to improve his game.

Sure, we naturally talk about golf, but Roscoe will somehow always connect it to some other aspect of our lives and encourage me to take everything in stride. When I make a great shot, he calmly praises it but gently reminds me not to get too excited—my next swing might send my ball into a sand trap.

Roscoe doesn't rest on his laurels or allow any of his accomplishments to inflate his ego because he says that life always finds a way to humble us eventually. "Enjoy it in the moment," he says, "but remember there will still be some tough shots ahead."

If I make a bad shot, he shrugs and says, "Don't worry; the next one will be better." With Roscoe, there is no need to compete, only to complete me, to build me up.

Which brings me to a friend of the past decade who serves not only as a friend but as a mentor, coach, and spiritual father. Bishop T. D. Jakes has always been someone I admired as a role model, appreciated as a man of God, and applauded as a brilliant entrepreneur and creative innovator. When our paths finally crossed at a ministry event, I admit I was a bit starstruck. By that point in my life, I had met enough of my heroes to know that their public persona did not always match their private personality. But Bishop Jakes immediately revealed himself to be the same man I knew him to be—warm and gracious, keenly intelligent and articulate, kind and generous.

Shortly after meeting him, I asked Bishop Jakes if he would be willing to mentor me, to help me be a better preacher, pastor, husband, father, brother, and friend. He looked in my eyes for a long time before speaking, probably only for sixty seconds but what seemed like sixty minutes! Finally, he asked me if I knew what I was asking for. In other words, entering into a mentoring friendship with him would not be merely a social, superficial, or surface relationship.

And that very quality—of being a truth-teller—is why his friendship has been and continues to be so important to me. Bishop Jakes has already been where I'm traveling and doesn't mind sharing everything he's experienced on a similar path—the good, the bad, and the ugly. He tells me what to look out for, what to expect, what to avoid, and what to make sure I don't miss.

His affirmation, admiration, and appreciation of me and my gifts mean more than I know how to express, providing me with a foundation of agape and phileo love that I missed growing up. Even when I don't hit the mark or take his recommendation, he tells me that he loves me, accepts me, and feels proud of me. This man's kudos and congrats are not easily attained, so when Bishop Jakes says it, I have no doubt he means it.

He's not afraid to challenge me, to offer me a different perspective, to shift my awareness beyond myself. He remains a friend willing to tell me when I'm right and when I'm wrong, loving me more than I'm able to love myself at times. He is one of many wise men who continue to bless me with their gifts.

CONNECTION IN CONTEXT

You may have noticed that I didn't use the term "best friend" for any of the gentlemen just described. I don't use the term because I don't find it particularly accurate or helpful in describing the kind of friendships that have enriched me the most. Your best friend on any given day often depends on your circumstances and their availability as well as their circumstances and your availability. There is nothing wrong with shifting your sense of connection and urgency based on context.

If you're starting a new business, then your best friend may be the one who just launched his own online retail site two years ago. If you're going through a divorce, then your best friend may be the one who has experienced similar pain before moving forward. If you're a new parent, then your best friends become the other parents who have gained invaluable wisdom and advice ahead of you.

This sense of contextual best works both ways. Some days we need something, which God provides through the unique contribution of a friend. Some days we are given an opportunity to love empowered, which God also provides through our friendships. Phileo love is about being a conduit, giving and receiving, being blessed to be a blessing, pouring out the love and resources you've been given in order to reflect God's agape love for those around you.

This model of empowered love enhancement is true with God as well. If you need to create something, then your Creator knows best what you need. If you need redemption, then Jesus is your ultimate relationship. And if you need comfort and the peace that passes understanding, then the Holy Spirit will provide for you.

This model of connection based on context is not the only way to consider phileo love, of course. To aid in my research for this book, I frequently asked family, friends, and loved ones how they would describe their beliefs and concepts of friendship. Many of the responses were similar to what we've already explored, but several stood out to me in the way they offered fresh insight and perspective.

My wife and I were enjoying a conversation with mutual friends when I posed my question, and one sister responded, "I see my friendships as an intricate system of relationships in a delicate ecosystem, similar to a particular geographic region and the life it supports. You won't find camels in the Arctic or penguins in the Sahara. Natural relationships spring up based on the kind of climate you create. As you develop various friends, you learn more about what you need to survive and thrive, and what you have to give others to fulfill their needs."

In contrast to her surprising analogy, a business friend of mine and I were enjoying lunch one day when he answered my question with a comparison that at first seemed predictable. "I think of my friends as part of my baseball team," he said and chuckled. "The players on my roster may vary from season to season and challenge to challenge, but they each share common qualities that contribute to my team." When I challenged his metaphor by gently inquiring about whether his friendships were only for his personal victories, he replied, "Not at all. I hope I provide the support, encouragement, resources, and team spirit that a good coach or general manager provides."

Finally, a friend in ministry shared his model based on the example of Jesus. He described how the larger his church and ministry grew, the more he received requests and opportunities for various friendships. Soon, he had hundreds of new friends, online supporters, and followers on social media, but he felt lonelier and more isolated than ever. So he began assessing whether his friends were companions or confidants.

He explained, "Companions are moving in the same direction you're going in, but they may not be going at the same speed or have the same destination in mind. They provide relational connections during our daily journeys for a season, but they're not necessarily lifelong pilgrims alongside us for the long haul. Those friends are confidants, and based on what Jesus demonstrated, I try to limit myself to no more than twelve of these deeper, more intimate friendships. And within my twelve, I pour more into and receive more from two or three than all twelve."

TETHERED BY LOVE

The final model of friendship I want to share from my conversations illustrates phileo love in a way that continues to resonate with me. An older gentleman who's been with our church since it started told me, "You've probably heard that the church should not be a place for the healthy but for the sick." I nodded as Jesus' words to the Pharisees came to mind: "It is not the healthy who need a doctor, but the sick. I have not come to call the righteous, but sinners" (Mark 2:17).

"A few years back, I was in the hospital, Pastor Keion," this gentleman continued, "when a nurse came in to change the IV bag containing the fluids and medications I needed for my recovery. I started thinking about how we all need friends willing to provide us with the love and support we need on a regular basis, just as they need what we can pour into their lives. I couldn't get the thought out of my mind and continued to reflect on this image of interdependence."

"That's a powerful illustration, brother," I assured him.

He smiled. "Well, it certainly stuck with me. I decided that 'I' stands for *intentional* and 'V' stands for *vulnerable*. And you don't want to be pouring into someone like a fire hose! You want to be consistent and steady. Just like the drip, drip, drip of an IV. Friends provide your IV regularly and you provide their IV regularly."

I have to say this image sums up the essence of what phileo love is all about. From my experience intentionality is a huge part of what sustains healthy friendships. If you just connect when circumstances allow or when it's convenient, then you will likely drift apart. Everyone is busy these days, most of us are exhausted, and many of us struggle to accomplish our roles and responsibilities.

The irony is that during these times we need the love, support, encouragement, and perspective of a real friend more than ever. So the only way to overcome the entropy of busyness is by prioritizing time, attention, and energy with the handful of friends who mean the most, the ones you need who need you. Being intentional means paying attention to details, going out of your way to know the day-in, day-out details of your friends' lives. Leaning in to hear what is spoken by their silence when you're communicating. Reading between the lines written by their words.

Vulnerability is also essential for the life and well-being of a phileo friendship. And I'll admit that this element causes discomfort for many people at various times, including myself. In a world that seems to threaten, troll, and trample our hearts and dreams, it seems wise to remain strong, stoic, and standoffish, guarding your-self against those who would learn your struggles, weaknesses, and challenges—only to use them against you.

If you remain defensive and guarded against almost everyone, however, you will never risk being known and accepted and loved for who you truly are, something every human being innately craves. In order to fulfill this longing, we must be willing to risk vulnerability—removing the masks of competency, success, achieve-ment, strength, and power and allowing others to see our inade-quacy, shame, failures, mistakes, weaknesses, and flaws.

Granted, you should not be vulnerable at the same level with everyone or even with all friends you trust. Phileo love is patient and willing to go slowly in getting to know someone, not forcing them to remove their defenses or sharing too much too soon. But the deepest friendships I have were forged by each of us being will-ing to risk openness, honesty, and candor with no expectations for benefiting in return.

This last caveat is significant because otherwise the risk is miti-gated in order to manipulate. It's the difference between being transparent and being vulnerable. Transparency allows others to see through your masks and defenses to a certain degree but not all the way. Transparency is typically transactional: You're being transpar-ent in order for the other person to reciprocate and remove their defenses. You're being transparent to appear compassionate, moral, righteous, accessible, and relatable.

Vulnerability, however, has no agenda beyond being known as you are. The other person might reject you, hurt you, abandon you, or exploit you. But you're willing to take that risk because you are tethered by the love of God.

Jesus showed us this kind of vulnerability and consistency and urged us as His followers to do the same:

My command is this: Love each other as I have loved you. Greater love has no one than this: to lay down one's life for one's friends. You are my friends if you do what I command. I no longer call you servants, because a servant does not know his master's business. Instead, I have called you friends, for everything that I learned from my Father I have made known to you. (John 15:12–15)

Because of the friendship Christ facilitates with us, we can share the same kind of sacrificial, selfless love that He embodies. We no longer have to posture and pretend to be someone we are not. Phileo love between friends requires laying down our own agendas, our egos, our pride, our selfishness, our fears, and our expectations. Phileo love becomes a picture of God's love enriching our lives beyond measure and enriching the lives of those around us.

CHAPTER 8

Family Matters

God made certain people part of your life because he knew his purpose for your lives will be achieved through your bond.

—Unarine Ramaru

Blest be the tie that binds," the old hymn says, "our hearts in Christian love."[1]

The ties we have to other believers are indeed blessed, although sometimes we have to make sure those ties don't bind too tight. The key is finding connections that keep us grounded without limiting our ability to soar. Spiritual friendships that allow us to be known and seen for who we really are—not who we have been conditioned to be by our appearance, our education, our career, our possessions, our wardrobe, the church we attend, our volunteer work, charitable giving, or any of the other props we use to hide behind.

Just as in your biological and chosen families, love within your spiritual family can be life-changing. Relationships with brothers and sisters in the faith can sharpen and sustain you, encourage and empower you, in ways that reveal the agape love of God unlike anything else in this world. I only have to consider the unconditional love and support I've received from my church family at the Light-House Church to know the significance of phileo in action.

I only have to think about a family I know who helps young adults rescued from human trafficking. They welcome these survivors of horrific abuse, most of them still adolescents, with patience, kindness, gentleness, and compassion. They let them stay for months, sometimes years, at a time, making sure they learn basic life skills necessary for self-care and independent living.

Or I recall the power of our church's community groups to come alongside one another and support their shared commitment to trust God during the tough times and praise Him together during the good times. Based on what I've experienced, observed, and heard from various members, the secret of their success comes from the power of love. The kind of love that refuses to judge, to gossip, to jockey for power or control, to compare, or to criticize. The kind of love that cooks and delivers meals for weeks when a family welcomes a new child into their home. The kind of love that listens, prays, comforts, and encourages. The kind of love that endures the pain of cancer treatments and chemo, of children in rehab and other loved ones battling addiction, of marriages strained to separation, of finances crippled by debt and undisciplined spending.

Jesus told us, "A new command I give you: Love one another. As I have loved you, so you must love one another. By this everyone will know that you are my disciples, if you love one another" (John 13:34–35). Not only do we obey our Savior when we love our brothers and sisters in Christ, but we also reflect and extend His love to those observing. When it comes to our relationships within the family of God, our phileo love becomes a mirror of our Father's agape, shining and magnifying His light into the world's darkness.

Now, perhaps more than ever, we have opportunities to let everyone know that we belong to Jesus by the way we love one another. Particularly within the family of God, we can let down our defenses, relax our performance posturing, and be seen and accepted for who our Creator designed us to be.

LET YOUR SPEECH REFLECT YOUR REACH

Believe me, I know this kind of love is not easier—in fact, I'm convinced that phileo love within the church often feels more challenging because of our expectations. We expect for those outside the body of Christ to sometimes misunderstand us, distrust us, criticize us, belittle us, and dismiss us. But when we experience some of the same treatment from those with whom we share spiritual bonds, the pain and disappointment cut deep. We want to believe we should always be treated fairly, justly, and honestly by others who say they share our same beliefs and faith practices.

The reality, though, is that even when sharing spiritual bonds within God's family, we are still human. We still have our issues and agendas, our tragedies and triumphs, our weaknesses and wanderlust. So perhaps we might reconsider our expectations if they seem to set us up for disappointment consistently. Simply put, phileo reminds us that we don't have to like someone in order to love them.

Even while commanding His followers to love one another, to realize others were watching and would assess them based on how they treated one another, Jesus was well aware of the lingering flaws in our humanity. Even among the twelve disciples, the men living with and serving Him, Christ experienced some of the same petty squabbles that can be found today. They even began comparing and apparently competing against one another, hoping to be more important than those around them.

With this mindset, the disciples asked Jesus, "Who, then, is the greatest in the kingdom of heaven?" (Matt. 18:1). After telling them that anyone wishing to enter God's kingdom must become like little children, Jesus warned them to be relentless in eliminating whatever causes one to stumble:

> If your brother or sister sins, go and point out their fault, just between the two of you. If they listen to you, you have won them over. But if they will not listen, take one or two others along, so that "every matter may be established by the testimony of two or three witnesses." If they still refuse to listen, tell it to the church; and if they refuse to listen even to the church, treat them as you would a pagan or a tax collector.
>
> Truly I tell you, whatever you bind on earth will be bound in heaven, and whatever you loose on earth will be loosed in heaven.
>
> Again, truly I tell you that if two of you on earth agree about anything they ask for, it will be done for them by my Father in heaven. For where two or three gather in my name, there am I with them. (Matthew 18:15–20)

What stands out in this passage is Jesus' emphasis on communication, particularly listening. Learning to listen plays an essential role in overcoming lazy love. Because lazy love goes out of its way to avoid clear, direct, open, and honest communication.

So much of loving those around us in the body of believers comes down to being present and attuned to the details of their lives, the burdens they're carrying, the needs spoken and unspoken, the joys shared and celebrated. Lazy love would rather focus on itself, barely registering what others are saying let alone being attuned to their hearts. Lazy love, detached from the agape source of God's limitless and unconditional love, needs constant filling from others. No matter how much other people pour in, though, it's never enough.

Shifting from this obstacle to a richer and more rewarding way of relating often begins with focusing on communication. You definitely want to walk what you talk. But it's just as important to let your speech reflect your reach!

LAZY LOVE HEARS BUT NEVER LISTENS

Communication is fundamental to loving others, including our brothers and sisters in the family of God. The problem arises, of course, in the clash of communication styles converging when there's a conflict. Just as we develop different attachment styles, based on our formative bonds with caregivers, in how we relate to others, we also communicate in distinct ways—particularly when it comes to conflict.

Like a cold air mass rushing into a warm weather front to produce an epic storm, conflicts often result over communication styles as much as isolated issues or problems. Part of the problem stems from how each stakeholder in a conflict perceives the size of what's at stake—for themselves as well as others. When there's a hint of conflict, some believers immediately try to disappear. They fear what they don't know how to do—to disagree in love and find ways to compromise and collaborate. Others enjoy talking about problems without any desire to contribute to solutions. And most people directly involved when opinions clash seem to listen to only themselves and those supporting their views. It's a funny thing, too, that most individuals can find some verse or passage of Scripture to support their position. And yet they rarely stop to pray and listen for God's response.

Often I suspect it's a matter of pride, a matter of power-posing, a matter of posturing just as the Pharisees tried to hide behind their performance as self-righteous exemplars of godliness. But within the family of believers, it's paramount that we lay down our pretenses and promotions, our theological training and church work, and our reliance on denominations and family history. We can simply be ourselves.

I suspect some individuals caught up in conflict might even view too much communication as part of the problem—too much talk, online and off the record, without anyone exchanging ideas openly. In many relationships, inevitable conflicts often produce a lot of noise playing louder and louder, as if volume alone might produce a victorious way forward. The key to communication, however, at least when it comes to conflict among our Christian sisters and brothers, is listening.

When we only talk over one another, when we speak based on untried assumptions and erroneous expectations, then the real messaging gets lost in the cloud cover. And the more clouds, the more obscure the sky becomes until it's hard to see the way forward. Jesus said, "My sheep listen to my voice; I know them, and they follow me" (John 10:27). I'm confident that when we listen with our hearts as well as our ears, we also recognize our Shepherd's love in the voice of our fellow believers.

The Bible has a lot to say about how we talk to one another. James urges us all to "be quick to listen, slow to speak and slow to become angry" (James 1:19). Paul references the importance of how we communicate to one another in his epistles to believers in the early church: "Do not let any unwholesome talk come out of your mouths, but only what is helpful for building others up according to their needs, that it may benefit those who listen" (Eph. 4:29). And my favorite: "Let your conversation be always full of grace,

seasoned with salt, so that you may know how to answer everyone"
(Col. 4:6).

Let's pause here for a moment and consider the elements of
Christian communication we know just from these three verses:

- Quick to listen
- Slow to speak
- Slow to anger
- Restraint of unwholesome talk
- Contains beneficial encouragement
- Full of grace
- Seasoned with salt
- Wise in contextual response

These are the ingredients in the recipe for reciprocal understanding between those practicing phileo love.

Lazy love, on the other hand, loves to hear only what it wants
to hear. Remember, lazy love hates conflict in relationships because
conflict requires letting go of self-interests and loving sacrificially
and selflessly. Lazy love communicates the same way it tends to
flow—in one direction. When our communication is fueled by lazy
love, we're basically delivering a monologue.

We might as well be looking straight into the imaginary camera
in the reality show of our lives, which is basically talking to ourselves.
Or perhaps you've watched plays and movies where actors speak
directly to the audience or camera, sharing their views, thoughts,
and feelings with no one but themselves listening—and we serve
as their silent witnesses. Similarly, we often deliver our own monologues without realizing that we're not responding to what others
have communicated; we're simply reciting our default scripted message. These lopsided dialogues might be what we say to others in

person, but they may also be what we post on Instagram, TikTok, and other social media through our comments.

These monologues garner attention for us, but they do not invite conversation.

And divinely inspired dialogue is required in order to create new solutions.

The kind of solutions that overcome posturing and performing—the threats of lazy love.

PART OF THE WHOLE

When we're quick to listen and slow to speak, we discover the ability to view other perspectives besides our own. Attuned to the Holy Spirit, listening with our hearts as well as our ears, we receive more than the words being spoken to us. We glimpse the faith, hope, and love of those sisters and brothers taking part in the larger conversation. We suspend our own agendas momentarily and hold them loosely, allowing for the possibility—not that we are necessarily wrong and others are right—but that we have not been seeing the full picture clearly.

The full picture for believers in the body of Christ takes into consideration what everyone needs for the comprehensive health of the entire body, not just select parts. And each part needs all the other parts to form a whole! God's Word makes this irrefutably clear:

Just as a body, though one, has many parts, but all its many parts form one body, so it is with Christ. For we were all baptized by one Spirit so as to form one body—whether Jews or Gentiles, slave or free—and we were all given the one Spirit to drink. Even so the body is not made up of one part but of many...If the whole body were an eye, where would the sense of hearing be? If the whole body were an ear, where would the sense of smell be? But in fact God has placed the parts in the body, every one of them, just as he wanted them to be. If they were all one part, where would the body be? As it is, there are many parts, but one body. (1 Corinthians 12:12–14, 17–20)

Within the body of Christ, you are a vital part. But not the only part or the most important part. Despite our human tendency to want to elevate certain parts of the body, we must remember that we form an interdependent, integrated whole, not an independent, separate collection of fragments. This passage emphasizes that God has intentionally created and united all parts to function together. So as we relate to and love our brothers and sisters, we must respect, love, and appreciate them not only as other human beings created in our Father's image but also love them with phileo love as spiritual siblings and joint coheirs with Christ.

Phileo love within the family of God requires a willingness to cooperate in order to collaborate. The word "cooperate" comes from the Latin and joins the prefix *co-*, meaning "together or jointly," with *operati*, meaning "to work or operate." So cooperating means that you learn to work together, to work jointly, to harmonize as a whole rather than remain discordant in competing parts.

"Collaborate" has similar roots from the Latin but implies that the needed work has already been agreed upon or is already in progress. Which is why I believe we must cooperate—come together in the same direction—in order to collaborate and create something new from our labors. This is what family members have done since Adam and Eve left the garden and settled to the east, forced to work the earth and face the consequences of their rebellious choice to eat the forbidden fruit and disobey God. In order to survive, family units had to depend on one another.

In our world of blended and chosen families, the biological family unit does not have to rely on its members for individuals to survive and thrive. But spiritual families do not have that luxury. Yes, we are individually saved and new creatures in Christ. But we are also adopted into the family of God when we accept Jesus' free gift of salvation and invite the Holy Spirit into our lives.

THE LOVE LANGUAGE OF COMPROMISE

Keeping this spiritual family connection front and center can provide clarity when conflict arises. Compromise often gets a bad rep, one that implies no one got what they really wanted in a forced negotiation. But the surprise of compromise in many cases is that more stakeholders can receive more benefits than they would have received originally. Compromise based on phileo love, and not lazy love, looks for solutions better than what had gone before.

I like to think of phileo-based compromise as one of the body of Christ's primary love languages. You're likely familiar with the concept of love languages—the ways we communicate, express, and receive love in our marriages and friendships. Some people feel loved through acts of service or from the power of encouraging words and affirmations. Others feel loved through the giving and receiving of gifts, both tangible and intangible, while some enjoy the physical connection of touch and affection.

Or perhaps compromise is not a love language in the church as much as it is a term that reflects a commitment to connect, support, and serve one another as brothers and sisters in Christ. This commitment is easier to describe than to practice and, like most kinds of love, requires intentionality. Lazy love wants us to think that unity, growth, and fellowship in the body of believers either happens or it doesn't—basically, a passive approach. But phileo love knows that we must activate our love by taking action.

The process begins by making connections with our Christian sisters and brothers. At our church we believe a person has a propensity to receive and extend love if they have at least seven relationships with other believers. We've studied and observed that if people come only for our worship or teaching, they tend to move on fairly quickly or drift away. If they're experiencing phileo friendships, however, they begin to feel anchored and secure in a community, in a church home.

When people connect within the church, they experience a richer sense of belonging, of purpose, and of shared values and goals. Their priorities align and they know how to encourage and support one another. They enjoy being together and learning what God has been revealing in each of their lives. This is the essence of the word *koinonia*, which we often translate from the Greek as "fellowship." But koinonia encompasses more than just interacting, socializing, or sharing church. Koinonia is basically the lifestyle within our spiritual family, which we find described so beautifully in the early church:

> They devoted themselves to the apostles' teaching and to fellowship, to the breaking of bread and to prayer. Everyone was filled with awe at the many wonders and signs performed by the apostles. All the believers were together and had everything in common. They sold property and possessions to give to anyone who had need. Every day they continued to meet together in the temple courts. They broke bread in their homes and ate together with glad and sincere hearts, praising God and enjoying the favor of all the

people. And the Lord added to their number daily those who were being saved. (Acts 2:42–47)

It's no coincidence that the first time koinonia is mentioned in the New Testament, it's in this very passage—the word translated as "fellowship." Koinonia is about fellowship but also supporting, upholding, and serving one another. When people in our life groups experience ups and downs, they know they are not alone. We minister to one another, both as the church and as individual parts of the church, to meet the needs we inevitably experience in various seasons of life. Sometimes these needs are physical—food, shelter, clothing, job skills, transportation—and many times these needs are emotional, psychological, and spiritual—comfort, acceptance, and prayer.

We are each called to minister to others according to our gifts, our talents, and our resources. We grieve each other's losses and celebrate one another's achievements. We work together to share God's love by serving others who do not yet know Him. This includes meeting practical needs in our communities as well as sharing the gospel message in relevant personal ways. People don't want to know how much you know until they know how much you care.

Loving others in the family of faith can be challenging, frustrating, and occasionally painful. Sometimes it seems even more painful because we expect better from those who call themselves followers of Jesus, and when they disappoint, fail, offend, or betray us, the discordant injustice glares brighter. Which is why it's vital to the health of the body of Christ that we overcome lazy love and show our phileo love to one another. In order to be all that God created us to be, both as His individual sons and daughters as well as His church, we need one another.

Phileo love, derived from our divine source of agape, bonds us with others in spiritual friendship. Relying on God's love for us rather than our own abilities or selfish limitations, we recognize the image of our Father and Creator within each individual we encounter. We respect human beings for the divine image they bear and open our hearts to other believers as brothers and sisters in the Spirit of God.

Without phileo love we posture defensively even in—and sometimes especially in—relationships with others in the body of Christ. This might look like self-righteousness and comparative holiness, an underlying judgmental attitude always scanning for the flaws and failures of others. This might look like hiding behind the role of martyr, putting everyone else's needs before your own to demonstrate your spiritual maturity and Christlikeness, only to harbor resentment and bitterness. It might result in avoiding conflict by putting a saccharine spiritual veneer on problems and personal clashes. Only when we practice phileo love can we live as equal members of God's holy family, learning and growing together, forgiving and loving each other, faults and all, just as He has loved us.

If you want to overcome lazy love, then practice giving and receiving the riches of phileo love with those who share your faith. Stop trying to impress them with your piety or your positions of leadership in the church. Let go of posturing and positioning yourself out of pride in your Christian performance.

Instead, let the ties of common spiritual beliefs and commitments connect you with strength and power. You can risk being vulnerable and known by those who also know firsthand the same gifts of grace. Blessed be those friendships in the fellowship of believers!

CHAPTER 9

Leaders and Authorities

People do not care how much you know until they know
how much you care.

—John C. Maxwell

Successful leadership is fueled by phileo love—not by authority, position, or power.

Because we tend to associate phileo with friendship, we often overlook how it applies to leadership and authorities. Like all forms of love, it flows both ways—how we respond with love to those who lead and have authority over us and how we respond with love to those we lead and have authority over. As long as those relationships run smoothly, practicing phileo love with intentionality may not come to mind.

Yes, there are often issues regarding how to define our relationships with leaders as well as our relationships with those we lead. Some leaders want others to know them, like them, and accept them, while others don't value their popularity or the opinions of team members. You have likely experienced the extremes of this spectrum, with a leader who tries hard to be considered humble, relatable, and accessible on one end, and a leader who sets firm boundaries to create distance, elevation, and awareness of authority on the other.

While elements of friendship often appear in the dynamics of authoritative leadership—including curiosity, respect, compassion, communication, and reciprocity—leaders are not required to be our friends, nor are we required to befriend those we lead. Friendship can, in fact, impede or dilute the power, authority, and respect required for leaders to flourish. In many workplaces, you might find friends in those who are peers in status, position, responsibility, and salary, but when the power balance shifts one way more than another, phileo love seems to disappear.

Either way, friendship isn't the determining factor of a great leader.

Posturing and propping up your authority as a leader doesn't work.

Phileo love defines great leadership.

HOUSTON, WE HAVE A PROBLEM

The moments that define the kind of leader we become are often those that challenge us to respect those in leadership above us. Those moments when we *react* internally with anger, confusion, frustration, disappointment, and shame but recognize our choice in how we *respond* outwardly with our attitude, words, and actions. This has certainly been my experience.

Included in the most obvious examples remains one that I now view as transformative. At the time, however, the situation left me disappointed but also struggling to understand what God might be doing in my life. A situation that initially appeared too good to be true proved just that—at least until it led to something even better than I could have imagined.

Early in my vocational ministry, shortly after college while I was still living in Indiana, I received an invitation from a large, well-respected church in Houston. The senior pastor of this church, highly regarded and much beloved, had announced his intention to retire within the very near future, setting in motion a pastoral search committee intent on finding his successor. After several conversations and an on-site visit, I was thrilled to learn that they felt the Lord had led them to me as their next senior pastor. Before accepting, I prayed, discussed it with my family, and consulted my spiritual mentors—all indicators led to Houston.

The move was a big leap for me, on many different levels. The church and its congregation were larger than where I had previously served. The responsibilities were of course greater as well. The size of the community there plus the scale of a major metropolitan city like Houston also weighed on me. As the details fell into place, though, I felt my apprehension melting into confidence at what I glimpsed God doing ahead of me.

Landing in Houston proved a little bumpy at first, but I rested in the certainty of why I was there—to answer the call God had placed on my life in this place where I felt led. Members of the congregation welcomed me with open arms and many kind gestures of acceptance. Best of all, or so it seemed, my predecessor would be continuing to serve during the transition, sharing his wisdom on the church he had been pouring his life into for many years.

During this season of passing the baton of leadership, I cannot recall struggling with respecting his authority and wisdom. As weeks began to drag out into months, however, I did grow impatient and a bit restless, eager to assume full responsibility for the leadership role I had been hired to assume. Soon, no one ever mentioned the retirement date that had been previously announced for the outgoing senior pastor. More and more, it simply seemed like business as usual with my elder remaining firmly entrenched and invested in all aspects of church life.

I consoled myself by thinking of David, the shepherd boy anointed by Samuel to be the next king of Israel following King Saul. Similar to my experience, David also had to endure a waiting period of patient endurance before eventually ascending to leadership. Surely I was experiencing a similar in-between time of preparation and equipping, even though I felt fully empowered for my position.

Only, it turned out not to be my position. The outgoing senior pastor reconsidered his decision and felt strongly that he would be leading indefinitely, making my role unnecessary. Although I had been well received and embraced as the future, the church members wanted the familiarity of the past maintained in the present. They were as kind as possible about changing direction, but I still struggled to wrap my mind around how I had ended up in this situation.

As I came to terms with this unexpected upheaval, I realized I had a choice to make, one that would have a direct impact on my faith, my future, and my friendships. I refused to allow anger or bitterness to poison the mixture of emotions swirling inside me. I embraced the disappointment and disorientation from this loss, and I made a conscious decision to accept, respect, and bless this church and its leader—who, technically, was still an authority, if not as my boss than as an older, more experienced man of God.

Phileo love in this situation arose out of my willingness to trust God. As much as I wanted to resent and withdraw from the new relationships I had formed, I dared to hope that somehow, someway God had something better for me. That this change in my future was no surprise to the author and finisher of my faith but was instead an opportunity for Him to surprise me with His goodness.

In hindsight, His gift is crystal clear—LightHouse Church! If I had not come to Houston, I would not have accepted the opportunity the Lord presented to launch a new church and a fresh ministry. I trusted God had brought me to Houston for a reason, just not the one I had assumed I was there to fulfill. Instead, I was led to establish the Lighthouse Church and Ministries within the walls of a school, with a small congregation of fewer than twenty-five members. From that seedling, we have become a mighty oak expanding to four locations with nearly twenty thousand devoted members!

If I had stayed at the church that originally hired me, I would have missed out on the enormous blessings and growth I experienced as a result of going through that desert valley of vulnerability. And I most definitely would not be the leader I am today!

BLAMING, SHAMING, AND GAMING

When faced with disappointment, disruption, or devastation, lazy love prefers to respond by blaming, shaming, and gaming. Instead of accepting losses or owning responsibility for how to respond, lazy love prefers to blame someone. I could have blamed the senior pastor of that church for changing his mind, for not knowing what he wanted, for not listening to what God wanted. I could have blamed the church leaders and search committee for not telling me that there was a possibility their present pastor might not leave. I could have blamed the congregation for choosing him over me.

Or, I could place my trust in the Lord and blame no one.

Rather than blaming, I could have allowed lazy love to shame me. Because this turn of events played into my insecurity and previous struggles with being seen, valued, and chosen. I had been pursued by a church back in Indiana prior to moving and told that I was one of two finalists. When it came down to their final selection, however, they chose the other pastor. The voice of lazy love, perhaps amplified and exaggerated by the enemy, whispered, "They didn't like you—you weren't good enough, strong enough, or mature enough in your faith. You will never be a pastor with impact or a leader with vision."

Or, I could listen to the Spirit of Truth and refuse to let shame linger.

If not blaming or shaming, then I could have gotten caught up in the mind games that lazy love delights in playing. Games that can't be won. Games that would send me ruminating over my past with regret rather than accepting the present and trusting God with my future. I was tempted to think that if I could figure out what I could and should have done differently, then maybe I could have stayed at that church and forced the other pastor to leave. If I had performed differently, I could have controlled the situation to rig the game of life in my favor.

Or, I could walk by faith and know God controls my destiny.

Because lazy love relies on our limited, human capacity for love, it refuses to rely on faith when confronted with obstacles. Because lazy love focuses on meeting our needs above everyone else's, it overlooks the impact it can have by giving instead of taking. Because lazy love would rather avoid the painful tension of not being able to see what God is planning and how we will fit into that plan, it gets stuck in place.

Lazy love wants to turn inward when hardships happen and withdraw, protecting and defending from the impact of painful emotions, unexpected losses, and events beyond your control. Rather than remaining rooted in the source of all love, the holy and almighty triune God, lazy love tries to conserve what it considers its limited supply of love. Lazy love then assumes the worst—about damage done, about people's motives, about unknown outcomes.

Loyalty is rejected when you sink into lazy love because it may result in even greater pain, discomfort, or inconvenience. Because loyalty requires swimming against the current of stormy waters, keeping your eyes fixed on Jesus, and trusting that He anchors you to solid ground. Lazy love claims to have your best interests at heart and keeps a tight grip on safety rather than sacrifice, on soothing rather than suffering, on standing still rather than stepping out.

Gratitude is also overlooked by lazy love's focus on what it lacks. Instead of being present and giving thanks for the blessings of today, love that's lazy always sees what's missing and assumes everyone else's grass must be greener. Lazy love constantly compares to make sure you always feel deprived, neglected, less-than.

But you have a choice. You know that love is much more than your feelings, and this is especially true for phileo love when those in authority over you make decisions that you don't like. When your boss takes credit for the hard work you put into a project, when your pastor asks you to serve behind the scenes, when your community leaders ignore your concerns, you must remember the choice you have to love actively—or to passively sink into the quicksand of lazy love.

However, please understand that, yes, there are times when you may need to challenge authority or question those in leadership over you. We will explore those situations in our next section, but you must be careful not to look for exemptions, justifications, and entitlements just because of the cost of obedience. Because choosing to love loyally, faithfully, and boldly is not merely what we are called to do as followers of Jesus. It is also an act of refusing to allow lazy love to rob us of peace, passion, and purpose.

Phileo love reveals just how much we have first been loved.

It humbles us and allows us to serve, to submit, to suffer, to sacrifice.

Never out of weakness—but always out of strength.

OCEAN OF UNCERTAINTY

There is another danger lazy love presents with regard to leadership and authority—sidestepping the responsibility when we are called, chosen, or forced to lead. It's easy to enjoy the perks of being in charge and accept the praise for goals attained when all goes smoothly. There is still a price to pay anytime you lead—and we are all called to lead in various capacities—but the greater the challenge you encounter as a leader, the greater the temptation to resort to lazy love.

I faced this temptation many years back when going through a divorce. Talk about a humbling situation! Any time a change of such magnitude takes place, the consequences ripple throughout all arenas of life. This is especially true regarding the areas where you lead or steward authority.

As a pastor charged with leading a vibrant church and growing ministry, I cringed inwardly thinking of how the fallout from my divorce would likely wreak havoc on all aspects of my responsibilities. Divorce remains an emotionally charged issue for many believers and an unpleasant reminder of their own struggles and failures for others. I knew without a doubt some people would judge me, reject me, gossip about me, and refuse to have anything to do with me. As the saying goes, the haters are going to hate no matter what, and now I was going to be front and center with an incredibly painful, tender, and vulnerable transition.

Thankfully, I didn't have to think twice about how to handle my disclosure: with humility, honesty, and especially hope. Hope that enough people would still care about me regardless of my marital status. Hope that enough people would be willing to extend love and grace to me at a time when I needed it most. Hope that even if members decided they did not want a divorced man to be their pastor, our church would survive and thrive nonetheless.

I'm not sure I have ever been more anxious, afraid, and antsy than when I announced my somber news before our congregation. The rapid beating of my heart became the only sound I could hear as I scanned familiar faces looking back at me in shock. Some people gasped, others whispered a prayer, and a few began to cry. Others remained stoic and revealed no emotion, either by choice or the conditioned response of their bodies to painful news.

That Tuesday evening I might as well have jumped off a cliff into a churning ocean of uncertainty. I felt led to step down from leadership. Thank God for the lead servants in our church who encouraged me to keep leading. They demonstrated phileo love in ways I had never experienced before. Modeling the example of Jesus, they refused to condemn, criticize, or compare. Throwing neither stones nor shade, they instead showered me with grace.

SHADES OF GRACE

Prior to my divorce, if you had asked me (or others, I suspect) to describe my leadership style, I (or they) would likely have responded with the words "strong," "authoritative," and "confident." After moving through this painful transition in my personal life, my leadership style has become both deeper and broader, both softer and firmer. I lead with more depth because of the depth to which I experienced the love of God and generosity of grace from others. My style has become broader because more than ever I want our church to be a place saturated with grace, welcoming anyone and everyone seeking to know God and experience His lavish love.

My leadership style is now softer because humility reminds me to lead with compassion and caring, to avoid the sharp edges of the world we live in, and to abstain from judging others. My authority is firmer, however, because of the confidence and certainty from which I lead, knowing without a doubt that God does not require perfection from His children, only an openness to His grace and goodness.

Before my divorce, I had no idea how many members were there because we were "doing well" and projecting the aura of biblical positivity they wished to exude. But this season of change, followed by the COVID-19 pandemic, made it clear that people came and stayed at our church because they experienced God's love, glimpsed His grace, and enjoyed community—a genuine sense of phileo love in action.

Not long after the dust began to settle, one member came to me and said, "Pastor, I want you to know that I've learned a lot from you and your example. I've realized just how important it is for a leader to have integrity. To share mistakes and challenges in front of those who follow you, well, that requires dedication, loyalty, and a deep faith in the Lord." His words brought tears to my eyes and a smile to my face.

Of course, there were some individuals and a few families who left, whether because of all I shared or for other reasons, I don't know. One departure in particular shook me, because this couple had been with us from the first day we opened our doors at Light-House. I felt the loss of their presence acutely because I had walked with them through a number of family turmoils and traumas. But they were unwilling to walk with me through mine. When they were in trouble, I ran toward them; when I was in trouble, they ran away.

By the sheer grace of God, our church not only retained the same level of members—we continued to grow! Without a doubt, I learned so much from this experience, one that I feared would destroy all that I had worked so hard to build in advancing God's kingdom. Instead, the Lord used this painful transition to demonstrate new depths of love and new shades of grace. I've learned firsthand that "grace" is a leadership term, not just a virtue made evident in people who are weak. The grace of phileo love that I experienced now permeates the way I seek to lead by serving. The way I lead now is based on grace laced with authority and love supported by God's truth.

When phileo love fuels you and propels you to lead, then you can exceed your human limits. You can be the leader you would love to follow. Be the leader you would love to serve. Be the leader you would love to work alongside.

TESTING LOYALTY

Going through that experience also taught me the value of trusting God even when I don't know what the outcome will be. When there's no certainty that things will turn out like I hope. When it's unclear what the next few days hold, let alone my entire future. Coupled with the way so many of our church members trusted me, I see the immense importance of trusting despite a lack of clarity.

My congregants knew without a doubt that I was trusting the Lord, so therefore they remained confident in trusting me. They revealed the importance of loving leaders because of their humanity, not in spite of it. Because humanity and its limitations cause us to rely on God's power and not our own. Even when nothing makes sense or we cannot grasp how God can use such painful circumstances to reveal His love.

When we lack phileo love, when we resist trusting God's love even if circumstances do not make sense, then we tend to disrespect leaders and authorities in our lives, either overtly or covertly. We may go through the motions of following directions, obeying rules and instructions, and working together, all while inwardly belittling their leadership by focusing on their inadequacies. We posture by pretending to be a team player or good soldier until there is an opportunity to rebel, to gossip, to disobey, to deny, to gaslight, or to advance by whatever means possible.

Phileo love with God as our source enables us to hold the tension necessary to love those in leadership and authority over us even when we disagree, do not understand, or doubt their motivations. We trust God and His omniscient leadership, not the human beings above us, with our futures. We know that He alone is in charge and provides power to obey as well as discernment for when to challenge decisions and policies that are human-made and not heavenly-made.

This kind of devoted trust reminds me of one of the most troubling incidents in all of Scripture—when God asked Abraham to sacrifice his son Isaac. We are told that God tested Abraham by instructing him, "Take your son, your only son Isaac, whom you love, and go to the land of Moriah, and offer him there as a burnt offering on one of the mountains of which I shall tell you" (Gen. 22:2 ESV). Without questioning or responding directly to God, Abraham proceeded to obey this unimaginable request.

Most people struggle with which is more shocking in this passage: God asking for a beloved son to be sacrificed as a burnt offering or a father apparently willing to obey such instruction. We could spend years and write numerous books on these two disturbing aspects of this event, and people have. But the essence of this situation can be distilled into two verbs: "tested" and "obeyed." God tested Abraham, and Abraham obeyed God.

Whether Abraham experienced fear, anger, resentment, outrage, or doubt, we are not told. Why God tested Abraham by asking for the most beloved gift in his life, his son, we are not told. What we are told is that Abraham got up early the next morning, saddled a donkey, and enlisted two young men to accompany him and his son on a journey. He cut wood to burn for the offering to God, and after three days they arrived in Moriah. Abraham gazed up to a mountaintop, told his helpers to stay put with the donkey, and bundled the firewood for his son to carry while Abraham carried the fire and a knife (see Gen. 22:3–6).

Obvious to Isaac, the main element for this sacrificial pilgrimage was missing—the lamb. So he asked his dad, "Behold, the fire and the wood, but where is the lamb for a burnt offering?" Rather than explaining what God had asked him to do, rather than alarming his son more than he might have already been, Abraham replied, "God will provide for himself the lamb for a burnt offering, my son" (Gen. 22:7–8 ESV).

Either Abraham's answer can be considered the ultimate elusive parental euphemism—along the lines of telling a child that someone who has died is only sleeping—or his answer reflects the unwavering faith this man had in the goodness and holiness of God. Regardless of how we view it, the scene proceeded to unfold in what can only be described as surreal terror meeting fearless trust:

When they came to the place of which God had told him, Abraham built the altar there and laid the wood in order and bound Isaac his son and laid him on the altar, on top of the wood. Then Abraham reached out his hand and took the knife to slaughter his son. But the angel of the LORD called to him from heaven and said, "Abraham, Abraham!" And he said, "Here am I." He said, "Do not lay your hand on the boy or do anything to him, for now I know that you fear God, seeing you have not withheld your son, your only son, from me." And Abraham lifted up his eyes and looked, and behold, behind him was a ram, caught in a thicket by his horns. And Abraham went and took the ram and offered it up as a burnt offering instead of his son. So Abraham called the name of that place, "The LORD will provide"; as it is said to this day, "On the mount of the LORD it shall be provided." (Genesis 22:9–14 ESV)

BASED ON LOVE

Yes, the disturbing questions and fearful anxiety this scene evokes are answered by the truth of Abraham's answer to Isaac's question—because the Lord did indeed provide. But not before Abraham raised the knife to sacrifice his son's life as God had instructed him to do. Only then, at the last possible moment, does the angel of the Lord intervene, affirming the father's obedient loyalty and protecting the son's life.

This incident gets our attention in ways that cannot be forgotten, dismissed, or fully understood. But what if that is the point here? What if God continues to ask us if we are willing to trust Him with who—and what—we love most? None of us can imagine sacrificing a child this way or complying with such an uncharacteristic request from our loving God.

But what if the consideration emerges as a test of our trust in God? Surely Abraham did not know based on his human logic what would happen in this scenario, that an angel would stay his hand and that God would provide a ram to be sacrificed instead of a boy. And yet Abraham obeyed because he believed that the God he knew, the One with whom he had made an everlasting covenant, would not allow such a horrendous sacrifice to be made without a redemptive reason.

Do we dare trust God with the same kind of bold, obedient faith that we see in Abraham when God asks us to give up what we love most? Isn't this the question that ultimately defines our love, that distinguishes lazy love from divine love? When we're faced with positive test results from the pathologist and don't see a ram in the thickets of radiation, will we trust God? When we're betrayed by the one person we had finally loved with all of our fragile heart—will we trust God then? When the unbearable, unthinkable, unimaginable happens and we face the loss of our child—to addiction or disease or incarceration—will we trust God then?

There is only one way for us to muster such faith—and it's based on love.

Not lazy love.

Supernatural, illogical, irrational, grace-laced love.

THREAT #3

Misunderstanding Affection due to Lack of Storge

Therefore, as God's chosen people, holy and dearly loved, clothe yourselves with compassion, kindness, humility, gentleness and patience. Bear with each other and forgive one another if any of you has a grievance against someone. Forgive as the Lord forgave you. And over all these virtues put on love, which binds them all together in perfect unity.

COLOSSIANS 3:12-14

To begin by always thinking of love as an action rather than a feeling is one way in which anyone using the word in this manner automatically assumes accountability and responsibility.

BELL HOOKS

CHAPTER 10

Heart of Stone

The opposite of love is not hate, it's indifference.

—Elie Wiesel

Airports are a great place to people-watch. I love observing the many different individuals, distinct groups, and unique expressions of our diverse humanity. Whenever I'm waiting at the gate or my flight's been delayed, I enjoy reading my fellow travelers.

I sometimes begin to imagine a narrative about their identity, reason for traveling, and destination. That older couple in matching polo shirts, with the husband trying to wrangle the wheelies of their carry-on luggage—I'm guessing they're headed to see grandkids in Dallas. Those three tall young women dressed in sweats and track jackets, traveling with only backpacks? They're teammates on a university basketball team. And that middle-aged frequent flier on his cell, looking fly in a navy bespoke suit? Founder of a start-up discussing that afternoon's agenda items with his personal assistant.

My favorite people in the terminal, of course, are families. Anytime I see a single parent juggling infants and preschool-age kids, I say a heartfelt prayer for peace, patience, and plenty of Pampers! Then there are families with older kids, who are likely traveling to see relatives at holiday time or to go on vacation together. If teens or young adults are part of the ensemble, then I can usually tell, along with everyone around them, whether they're glad to be there or not.

The most revealing scenes with families tend to be the ones involving homecoming. With the ability to text upon arrival, most travelers no longer have spouses, kids, or siblings waiting for them in the terminal and instead head to passenger pickup. Occasionally, however, I'll notice a group buzzing with excitement as they anticipate the return of a beloved family member, presumably after a long trip or extended absence.

I observed one such reunion recently when a young woman in military uniform disembarked to find a cluster of family and friends cheering, holding homemade signs, clapping and crying with joy. Hugs, tears, and affection were amply distributed among the dozen people who rejoiced to have their beloved daughter, sister, and friend back in their midst. I almost felt embarrassed for witnessing a scene of such familial intimacy.

The last time I flew, though, I witnessed a scene on the opposite end of the welcome-home spectrum. A disheveled-looking man, clearly fond of tats and piercings, perhaps in his late twenties, entered the main terminal and walked up to a trio apparently waiting for him. There was no happy chatter or excitement, only a half-hearted hug from the woman I assumed was his mother and a stiff handshake from a scowling, impatient-looking father figure. The third member of this less-than-enthusiastic welcome party appeared to be a younger brother, who did not even look up from his phone. Before they began shuffling toward baggage claim, voices were raised—quite a feat in the noisy ambience of an airport, and I distinctly heard the weary passenger shout, *"Why did you even come then?!"*

While there's no way of knowing the actual dynamics at play, or whether these people were even related to one another, I felt a pang of compassion for all parties in this tense tableau. Families are usually one of God's greatest blessings in life, but they can also be the source of lifelong struggles. Because as much as we want to love each other, we also have to bear the suffering of one another's sins.

And our body language often speaks louder than our words.

How we view the economy of affection often determines our relational wealth.

WISHFUL THINKING

Of the four kinds of biblical love, storge may at first seem to be the easiest and least complicated variety. Simply put, it's healthy affection. While the word "storge" is not found in the ancient languages used in Scripture, the concept clearly abounds. Storge derives from the Greek word *philostorgos*, a concept we might translate as "affection" or, more literally, as "tenderly loving." It's often used to describe the kind of natural, loving attention and responsiveness inherently found in families, in our biological families as well as those blended and chosen.

In many ways, storge takes us back to considering our attachment styles—those ways of loving that we experienced and then learned to act on going back to our earliest years. Ideally, we had parents and caregivers who gave us the kind of attention, affirmation, and affection God designed us to receive in order to mature into healthy, balanced, well-adjusted, interdependent men and women.

In reality, though, we know that such perfect attachment does not exist. We all have ways we can improve upon how we relate to and practice loving those around us. Otherwise, we leave ourselves to the default decay of lazy love. In fact, looking at storge's opposite condition sheds considerable light on the consequences of lazy love carried to its extreme.

You might recall that we find storge's antonym in the original Greek used in the New Testament. Paul used the word *astorgous* to describe godless people "who suppress the truth by their wickedness" and incur God's wrath (Rom. 1:18). This negative concept is not merely describing our sinful nature and selfish inclinations. Paul's talking about hard-core sinners intent on rejecting God and elevating themselves—and facing grave consequences.

These people "exchanged the truth about God for a lie" and were "filled with every kind of wickedness, evil, greed and depravity" (Rom. 1:25, 29). Rather than exercising the kind of love found in healthy families, these opposing individuals become "gossips, slanderers, God-haters, insolent, arrogant and boastful; they invent ways of doing evil; they disobey their parents; they have no understanding, no fidelity, no love, no mercy" (Rom. 1:29–31).

Such extreme godlessness may sound like hyperbole, but you only have to surf online for a few moments to realize that even today we live in a culture that encourages us to seek pleasure, self-fulfillment, and autonomous wealth at any cost. Social media has democratized the ability to be a celebrity in our own minds, in our own worlds, gauging our success by our number of followers. Please understand that I am not categorically denouncing wealth, contentment, pleasure, and social media; I am simply pointing out that the kind of inward hardness of heart described by Paul is alive and well.

Very few people, if any, would deliberately choose to harden their hearts, reject God, and suffer the results. No, the process is much more gradual than that. Hard hearts happen when love is lazy, and lazy love further hardens our hearts. This cycle creates a vortex that can be challenging, and may even feel impossible, to break out of on our own. As we will see in the next chapter, we ultimately need the power of God's Spirit in our lives to soften our hearts of stone into hearts of flesh.

But we also have to do our part in order to avoid drifting from God and allowing our hearts to become callous to the things of God. Like the proverbial frog in the pot of water that doesn't realize the temperature has gone up until it's boiling, we must pay attention to the state of our hearts long before they harden into stone.

How we give and receive affection provides a telling barometer of how we practice storge love. Beginning with our primary love relationship—with God—and extending to our families, friends, and other loved ones, we can use four indicators to assess the tenderness of our hearts: prayer, honesty, boundaries, and forgiveness. Each of these indicators is reflected in our willingness to connect with others, whether through an embrace, shared laughter, or the comfort of leaning on one another.

YOUR HEART'S DASHBOARD

Imagine driving your car down the highway one day when an indicator light pops up on your dash screen. Depending on the age and kind of vehicle, your indicator may simply be a shape or symbol or it might be a specific written message informing you of the problem. Either way, you know that something needs attention in order for your car to continue to function properly.

It could be something as minor as needing more window-washer fluid. Or it could be an indicator that the engine is running low on oil or transmission fluid. If you drive an electric vehicle, it might mean a short has occurred or that your battery needs recharging. Left unattended, the problem does not go away but usually leads to more serious—and costly—problems. I remember one friend of mine in college who used to take black electrical tape and place it over the indicator light rather than take his old car in for service.

Consider your heart working in similar fashion. Each day you may have indicators pop up to signal that regular care and maintenance is required. Ignored, you risk jeopardizing your physical, mental, emotional, and spiritual health. When monitored and addressed, however, you ensure that your capacity for loving from a well-tuned heart continues.

The place to begin is with this monitoring process itself. Being in relationship with God means making time with Him a priority every day. Nurturing this relationship requires constant communication, as evidenced by the instruction in God's Word to "pray without ceasing" (1 Thess. 5:17 ESV). Such constant communication may sound daunting at first, but think about how you remain connected to your spouse, your kids, your parents, or close friends. You don't need to be with them or talking with them 24-7 in order to maintain a strong bond of attunement. But you do need to check in with them frequently, perhaps daily, to share your lives and inquire about each other's well-being.

Similarly, you don't have to be on your knees, in church, or in your prayer closet 24-7 in order to maintain your direct connection to God. He is already with you, dwelling in your heart through the presence of the Holy Spirit. Learning to pray without ceasing is about attunement. Checking in with the Spirit throughout your day is easier than you may realize—it simply requires intentional practice.

As you're enjoying your morning coffee, thank Him for the new day ahead of you. If there's time, spend a few minutes praising and worshipping God before presenting to Him your requests and intercessions for others. Pray on your way to work. Before the big Zoom meeting, ask for divine power to help you focus. Picking up the kids from practice, pray for them or even ask them to pray with you. Give thanks before starting your evening meal. Reflect on the day's blessings as you prepare for bed.

The more you make talking to God a natural reflex, the more you keep your heart open and aware of His loving presence. This openness allows you to listen to Him as well, to be aware of His guidance and instruction, to resist temptation, to be reminded of His mercy and grace. Let prayer become the catalyst for recognizing other indicators, other areas that need attention in order to love boldly. Make the psalmist's prayer your own: "Search me, O God, and know my heart: try me, and know my thoughts: And see if there be any wicked way in me, and lead me in the way everlasting" (Ps. 139:23–24 KJV).

Prayer facilitates the fuel that keeps your heart filled with storge love.

Praying for those you love prevents you from becoming distant and aloof with them and their needs. When you pray with your petitions for other people, you are practicing a way of loving them that's reflected physically as well as spiritually. Sometimes this looks like holding hands while you pray, laying hands on someone's shoulders or head, pulling them in for a hug and a blessing. The posture of your heart toward them shows in your body.

OH, NO—FOMO!

Prayer and attunement to God's Spirit also keeps us honest—before the Lord and other people. When we focus on the truth of God's Word and keep our communication with Him consistent and connected, then we learn to detect the lies that seek to blind us and to bind us. If you glance back at Romans 1, you'll notice Paul emphasized that our hearts grow hardened when we exchange the truth of God for the lies of the enemy.

Once again, most of us don't wake up one day and decide to make that kind of erroneous exchange. The enemy is much too shrewd to confront us with lies so brazen we would immediately recognize them and flee. Instead, the devil becomes a student of who we are and how we live, focusing in particularly on our fears—including one that seems more rampant now, thanks to social media, than ever before: the fear of missing out.

FOMO is that feeling you get when you see several of your friends posting pics at an event that you didn't know about. Why didn't someone invite you? What's up with that? Did they intentionally leave you out? Or, perhaps worse, no one thought to include you. You may also experience FOMO when you realize you have several social opportunities occurring at once. There's no way you can be present at all of them so you're forced to choose—and sometimes obligated to choose a family gathering over what appears to be something that's much more fun, such as a barbecue, ball game, or birthday party.

Regardless of its source, FOMO plants seeds of insecurity, doubt, resentment, and bitterness in the garden of our minds. The enemy likes to churn up these emotions until there's a riptide inside you that grows stronger and more powerful. If you ruminate on them enough, you can convince yourself that you don't belong, that others don't really want your friendship, that you're basically all alone in your misery. Soon lazy love takes root as you move away from God and other people.

As contemporary as it seems, though, FOMO is nothing new. Ever since the serpent tempted Eve and Adam in the garden of

Eden, he's been playing mind games by exploiting our fears that there's more we could—and should—be enjoying. Notice how the enemy plants doubt by asking a question rather than taking a direct approach:

> He said to the woman, "Did God really say, 'You must not eat from any tree in the garden'?"
> The woman said to the serpent, "We may eat fruit from the trees in the garden, but God did say, 'You must not eat fruit from the tree that is in the middle of the garden, and you must not touch it, or you will die.'"
> "You will not certainly die," the serpent said to the woman. "For God knows that when you eat from it your eyes will be opened, and you will be like God, knowing good and evil." (Genesis 3:1–5)

The devil made Eve and Adam feel like surely they must be exceptions to God's warning. And by refuting what God had said about the consequences of eating this particular fruit, the serpent called God a liar. What irony, right? The father of lies, the devil, loves to twist the truth so that we feel like God's commands and instructions apply to everyone else but us. That God's holding out on us and keeping us from enjoying something that won't hurt us, some fruit that will be fun or pleasurable or thrilling or satisfying.

How can we avoid such lies? By saturating our minds and hearts with the truth of what God says—about who we are, about who He is, and about what's best for us. By facing our fears and accepting that we indeed may be missing out on something we might enjoy—at least temporarily. By refusing to believe the lies that allow us to justify being the exception. By refuting the enemy's lie that God cannot be trusted.

When we keep our hearts' GPS set on truth, it's much harder to stray from the narrow path.

BOUNDARIES AND BORDERS

On the other hand, when we buy into the enemy's lies and allow our fears to go unchecked by truth, we justify being dishonest with the people in our lives. Fueled by fear, we decide that we need to exaggerate our accomplishments, our achievements, our celebrity connections, our personal wealth. Fueled by insecurity, we decide to omit the facts that don't fit our image and brand so that we control what we allow others to see. Fueled by self-preservation and advancement, we decide to alter the boundaries of truth so that we can draw our own borders rather than staying within the lines of God's truth.

When I think about the ways we compromise the truth because of our fears, I remember Abraham. This patriarch of faith, even after entering into covenant with God, was still susceptible to fear-fueled deception. Following the destruction of Sodom and Gomorrah (see Gen. 19) and just before the birth of the son God promised him (see Gen. 21), Abraham and his wife, Sarah, moved into the land of Gerar. There, "Abraham said of his wife Sarah, 'She is my sister,'" which resulted in King Abimelek sending for Sarah to become his wife (Gen. 20:2).

God then warned Abimelek through a dream that taking Sarah would result in death because she was already a married woman. Abimelek pleaded with the Lord, maintaining that he went after Sarah with "a clear conscience and clean hands" because Abraham said Sarah was his sister (Gen. 20:5). God confirmed this and instructed the king to return Sarah to her rightful husband despite Abraham's deception. Obeying God, Abimelek returned Sarah and asked Abraham why he would lie about such a serious matter, to which Abraham replied:

> I said to myself, "There is surely no fear of God in this place, and they will kill me because of my wife." Besides, she really is my sister, the daughter of my father though not of my mother; and she became my wife. And when God had me wander from my father's household, I said to her, "This is how you can show your love to me: Everywhere we go, say of me, 'He is my brother.'" (Genesis 20:11–13)

Coming clean about the whopper of a lie he told, Abraham explained that he had assumed that because God was not feared in that land, the local inhabitants would kill him in order to take his wife. From there, he backtracked a bit by explaining that technically Sarah was his sister since they had the same father, and that he had pressured Sarah into going along with it out of her love for Abraham. That's a tactic I suspect we've all heard before at some point: "If you love me, then you'll lie for me . . . steal for me . . . do whatever I need you to do for me."

Notice Abraham's progression from assumption (the locals don't recognize my God) to fear (because they don't recognize God sent me, then they will harm me) to deception (I'll claim Sarah is my sister instead of my wife). Abraham shifted the boundaries of truth in order to protect himself, not trusting that God had gone before him to guard him and his household. Abraham also compromised Sarah, pressuring her to prove her love by going along with the lie, which he justified as a half-truth.

Thankfully, God intervened directly before further consequences ensued. Otherwise, the situation would have become even more complicated and dangerous. When we refuse to trust God and instead take matters into our own hands, we create false boundaries and compromise relationships. We assume we must rely on our own power and use lazy love as a bargaining chip as well as a shield. When we trust God and tell the truth, however, even while fearing the outcome, then we honor storge love.

Affection is never a bargaining chip in our relationships.

DON'T SLOW THE FLOW

Without storge love in our lives, we cut off part of our divine capacity to love by what we do. We attempt to reduce love to rules and regulations, to obligations and codependence, to hidden self-sufficiency at all costs. Our words and actions may reflect what others interpret as love from us, but we secretly harden our hearts and refuse to surrender our truest and tenderest selves to others. We misunderstand what it means to love both God and others, because we rely on the flawed examples and divine deficits we have experienced.

Perhaps the greatest way to honor storge love is by allowing our hearts to be both a receptor and a conduit for forgiveness. Otherwise, we experience a blockage that slows the flow of blood from our hearts to the rest of the body of Christ. We harbor grudges and allow resentment to blossom into bitterness, which then leads to entitlement, prejudice, self-righteousness, and hatred of those we are called to love.

Forgiveness is essential to maintaining an open, loving, grace-dispensing heart. When we refuse to forgive others or to own up to how we have offended them, we limit our ability to receive the grace God so freely gives. After His disciples asked Jesus to teach them to pray the way they had overheard Him praying, He led them in what we now know as the Lord's Prayer (see Matt. 6:9–13). In this concise model for prayer, Christ instructs us to ask our Father to "forgive us our debts, as we also have forgiven our debtors" (Matt. 6:12).

I know personally how failing to forgive can result in a hardened heart. You'll recall that I did not learn the identity of my biological father, the pastor at our church, until I was entering adolescence. While he refused to publicly acknowledge me as his son, my father did try to be a positive presence in my life from then on. He acted as a kind of mentor and tried to guide me into young manhood.

Because of the circumstances, however, I didn't want to trust his advice even when I suspected he was right. My ongoing bitterness and refusal to forgive him prevented me from enjoying the relationship we could have had if only I had been willing to let go of what we lacked. I remember one time in particular, when I was about nineteen and told my father about my interest in a certain young woman. When I told him I planned to date her, he said, "I wouldn't do that if I were you." He then explained what he had observed about her character, her circumstances, and her family.

Of course, you know what I did next, don't you? Asked her out the next day! This began a two-year period that eventually resulted in a painful breakup as what my father had warned me about came to light. But my angry rebellion also strained my already tenuous relationship with my dad. Despite the less-than-ideal situation with his paternity kept from the public, he was still my father—and deserving of the kind of storge love, honor, and respect our relationship afforded.

We eventually did grow closer before he passed away but not until I became aware of my need to forgive him and looked to my heavenly Father for what I had not received from my earthly dad. My lack of forgiveness cost me precious time that I could have spent growing closer and learning from the man who gave me life.

Instead, I allowed my hardened heart to block the flow of God's love in both our lives.

Left unattended, lazy love can metastasize into hard-hearted indifference and self-indulgent entitlement. Walking by faith and loving others, ourselves, and God requires a heart tenderized by compassion, grace, and mercy. A heart of flesh, not of stone, free to experience storge love flowing both inward and outward. Giving and receiving appropriate affection in ways that allow the body to demonstrate the tenderness and compassion of our hearts.

CHAPTER 11

The Hidden Heart

We must combine the toughness of the serpent with the
softness of the dove, a tough mind and a tender heart.
                    —Dr. Martin Luther King Jr.

I t's easy to take your heart for granted until there's a problem.
When you're young and healthy, you tend to assume your body
will remain strong and function smoothly. When everything is
working properly, there's no reason not to believe this. Unless there
are issues of concern with your cardiac health, you may not even
know how the heart does what it does.

You may not know (or remember from high school biology)
that the human heart is a vital organ about the size of a large fist
beating approximately 100,000 times each day in order to pump
roughly one and a half gallons of blood per minute throughout
the 60,000 miles of blood vessels in your body. At the center of
your circulatory system, the heart supplies oxygen and nutrients
to your tissues while removing carbon dioxide and other wastes. If
your heart doesn't do its job, your tissues and organs lose nourish-
ment and shut down.[1]

The two greatest threats to the heart's performance are blockage in any of its arteries, resulting in damage to the muscle; and

cardiac arrest, a sudden loss of functionality often caused by electrical irregularity affecting the heart's rhythm. A heart attack can cause cardiac arrest, but the heart's electrical rhythm can be disrupted by other causes, too.

Numerous treatments to alleviate blockage and hardening of the heart's arteries are available today, including medications and surgical procedures. While these may seem like relatively new methods, the first open-heart surgery in the US was actually performed in 1893 by Dr. Daniel Hale Williams, our country's first African American cardiologist, who also founded the first interracial hospital (Provident Hospital in Chicago) and cofounded the National Medical Association.[2]

While both the science and the history of the human heart help us appreciate this intricate organ, the heart provides a powerful metaphor for love that's even older. Just as the heart muscle can suffer injury, deteriorate, and atrophy, your capacity for love can do the same. All the more reason to learn and practice ways you can keep your metaphoric heart just as strong and tender as this essential muscle in your body.

HEART TRANSPLANT

Ancient Greek philosophers associated the heart with the strongest human emotions, particularly love.[3] At a basic level, this makes sense because what happens when someone feels attracted to another person? They experience a physical reaction that parallels what they feel. Their heart beats faster, supplying more oxygen to the rest of their body, which requires more as it becomes aroused. This arousal is not necessarily sexual but a heightened awareness of the body's senses, similar to the fight-or-flight response. As your pulse races and your blood pressure goes up, you can't help but notice the activation of your heart.

Prior to the ancient Greeks, however, the Bible mentions the heart and uses it figuratively more than one thousand times.[4] While the heart represents a variety of aspects of our humanity in Scripture, it primarily refers to the center of who we are—emotionally, intellectually, and spiritually. Just as the physical heart is not visible externally, the biblical heart is usually hidden, or not visible to other people, as well.

When Samuel went to anoint God's next king of Israel, he did not dismiss David—the youngest son of Jesse—as a contender, because "the LORD does not look at the things people look at. People look at the outward appearance, but the LORD looks at the heart" (1 Sam. 16:7). Jesus pointed out, however, that our words tend to reveal what's hidden in our hearts (see Matt. 12:33–34), which is also manifest by what we value and prioritize: "For where your treasure is, there your heart will be also" (Matt. 6:21).

Because our human heart remains tainted by a sinful inclination to serve ourselves, when we experience salvation, we are given a new heart through the power of the Holy Spirit (see Acts 15:9). Even before God sent Jesus as the means for us to know Him and experience His grace, God often used His prophets to contrast the hard hearts of people who had turned away from him with the tender hearts of those who knew and loved Him. Through the prophet Ezekiel, God declared, "I will give you a new heart and put a new spirit in you; I will remove from you your heart of stone and give you a heart of flesh" (Ezek. 36:26).

As we have already explored, the basis for this heart transplant is God's agape love for us. We love because He first loved us. Evidence of our new hearts is displayed in storge love, the physical and emotional ways we show caring, compassion, and affection to those people we consider family. In order to overcome lazy love, we must guard against the hardening of our hearts and do our best to keep them open, tender, and generous.

Which, like so many aspects of real love, is easier said than done—but not impossible.

BLESSED ARE THE LOVERS

Fortunately for us, though, we have the example of Christ on which to model the ways we love. We also have His instructions, which I'm convinced provide some clear practical principles on how we can keep our hearts from growing hard—not only toward God but also toward one another. As part of what we now call the Sermon on the Mount (see Matt. 5), Jesus taught His followers a series of cause-and-effect blessings that still resonate for us today:

Blessed are the poor in spirit,
    for theirs is the kingdom of heaven.
Blessed are those who mourn,
    for they will be comforted.
Blessed are the meek,
    for they will inherit the earth.
Blessed are those who hunger and thirst for righteousness,
    for they will be filled.
Blessed are the merciful,
    for they will be shown mercy.
Blessed are the pure in heart,
    for they will see God.
Blessed are the peacemakers,

for they will be called children of God.
Blessed are those who are persecuted because of righteousness,
     for theirs is the kingdom of heaven. (Matthew 5:3–10)

You have likely encountered these beatitudes previously, perhaps in sermons or messages intended to encourage you during hardships. But allow me to suggest a different perspective on these verses, as a paradigm for overcoming lazy love by preventing our hearts from hardening. Because I believe the beatitudes can be summed up as "Blessed are the lovers who love like God loves you"—and the key to loving like God involves the posture of our hearts. So if you will please indulge me, here is how Jesus instructs us to be better lovers:

- Practice humility (like those poor in spirit) in order to be a caretaker of the kingdom.
- Suffer your losses (like those who mourn) in order to provide and receive comfort.
- Be gentle (like those who are meek) so you can experience the fullness of love.
- Fight injustice (as those who hunger and thirst for righteousness) to create change.
- Show mercy (as the merciful) in order to reflect the mercy you receive from God.
- Be open, honest, truthful, and vulnerable (like those pure in heart) as an anchor to faith.
- Bring peace (like the peacemakers) as representatives of God's peace.
- Accept persecution (like those persecuted because of righteousness) as part of the struggle to love boldly.

These statements are obviously my interpretation, more of a paraphrase than any kind of direct translation. But these lessons on loving illuminate the process of showing the kind of compassionate affection that's the essence of storge love. Let's unpack them and consider their relevancy in our lives, particularly as we keep our hearts open, engaged, and tender with the group of people we love as our family, whether biological, adopted, chosen, or discovered.

FEEL YOUR WORTH

Humility, the quality of being poor in spirit, is probably not what you think it is. Because so many people seem to believe that being humble essentially means always putting others ahead of yourself, ignoring or suppressing your own needs, and letting others bulldoze over you. But biblical humility is all about knowing your identity and worth as God's child despite past conditioning, present commentary, or future uncertainty. I suspect we often view humility as a way of negating ourselves and our needs in response to experiences from childhood.

When we consider the way loving parents establish secure attachments with their children, showing and telling them their value is fundamental. It's how you and I learned who we are. Ideally, this relied on being loved simply for being ourselves—not how well we complied and conformed; not how much we achieved or accomplished; not how little we caused conflict or embarrassment.

Unfortunately, few people received a rock-solid awareness of their God-given value while growing up. Coupled with the messages we accept about ourselves from other family members, teachers, coaches, pastors, and peers, we often lose sight of the truth of just how special, unique, and beloved we are. God's Word tells us we are wonderfully and fearfully made, that we were worth sending His Son to die for us so that we could know the fullness of His love.

There's that great lyric in one of my favorite Christmas carols, "O Holy Night,"[5] which tells us, "Long lay the world in sin and error pining / 'Til He appeared and the soul felt its worth." Because God is the source of our love, our soul knows its worth. And because we know our worth, we don't have to impress others with pretentions and pretenses, playing games where we strive to appear one-up because internally we're feeling one-down.

If you struggle with how to show kindness, caring, and affection to your loved ones, then hit pause and consider what's blocking you. Could it be that you want to give as little as possible in order to get as much as you think you need from them? Perhaps this expresses itself in the way old sibling rivalries continue to create distance between you and your brothers and sisters. Maybe you refuse to forgive your parents and continue to hold them responsible for what you failed to receive as a child—even though you are now an adult capable of stewarding your own needs. Regardless of what impedes your ability to love, humility knows its worth and sees others with the same divinely appointed, worthwhile value.

GIFTS OF COMFORT

Suffering your losses—that is, being willing to grieve—also requires an awareness of your soul's worth. So often, we struggle to walk through the emptiness loss leaves behind because we fear we will be consumed by that ache, that void of sadness. Rather than express our need for comfort, for love, for the presence of others who care about us, we retreat into ourselves and withdraw. As we isolate our grief, we often feel stuck in it, unable and unwilling to acknowledge and express just how much another person, a relationship, a home, or a family member meant to us.

But unless we're willing to suffer life's losses, we miss out on one of the most powerful aspects of storge love—comfort. One of the greatest lessons I've learned as a father is how to comfort my children through my presence rather than by trying to fix, distract, or dismiss their losses. As much as I want to take away their suffering and grief, the truth is that being with them in it is often much more challenging. Because sharing space for us to grieve and comfort one another requires a willingness on my part to feel the depths without trying to fix something that ultimately cannot be compensated.

If you want to grow closer to your family members, then recognize the gifts of comfort you can offer simply by showing up, by acknowledging what or who has been lost, and by holding them. Some of the most powerful moments I've shared with my family members have occurred without either of us saying a word. Instead, our hearts lean in toward one another, aware of our shared pain, and find comfort because we are not alone in our loss.

Suffering our losses in order to give and receive comfort is also a powerful way to practice being *gentle and merciful*. I prefer "gentle" to "meek" because of the distinction between our associations. Similar to the way we tend to misunderstand humility, "meekness" is one of those words that sound holy and biblical but far too weak and vulnerable to actually practice. Some people I've talked with define meekness as being shy and passive, almost afraid to step up, and committed to avoiding confrontation.

Outside of the church, being merciful can also sound like you're giving in or giving up on holding someone accountable. Rather than just letting them off the hook, however, both gentleness and mercy require immense strength and power. And there's no better example of this kind of strength and power than how we see Jesus being gentle and merciful to those who needed it most.

While dying on the cross, Jesus saw His mother and His beloved disciple, John, and instructed them to take care of one another (see John 19:26–27). To have such consideration while being tortured to death shows incredible fortitude and love for His family members.

Prior to His death by crucifixion, Jesus also showed great mercy to one of the criminals being punished beside Him (see Luke 23:40–43). While the criminal on the other side of Christ mocked Him, the penitent thief pointed out that he and the other thief deserved their punishments because of their crimes, but Jesus was innocent and suffering the same death. This criminal then asked Jesus to remember him when Christ came into His kingdom, to which Jesus replied, "Truly I tell you, today you will be with me in paradise" (Luke 23:43).

This is the kind of muscular meekness and mercy we need in our relationships with those we love most. I'm reminded of a dear sister, a lifelong friend of our family, who was abused by her alcoholic stepfather when she was a child. After many years in her adult recovery, this woman made the courageous decision to have a conversation with both her mother and her stepfather, now sober for a decade and an active church member.

Our friend expressed her decision to forgive her abuser and then outlined the steps required for rebuilding their relationship going forward, which was something both her parents had frequently requested. I am not saying this is the only way to handle such painful, complex relationships, but in this woman's case, she put her faith into action by releasing her anger and defensiveness and choosing to forgive—and to reestablish some kind of relationship.

Rather than allow her heart to harden, she chose a path of courageous compassion.

DISAGREE TO AGREE

Fighting injustice and *bringing peace* are also ingredients for tender-izing our hearts. At first glance, these two may seem to be at odds with one another, but I have paired them for that very reason—just as I suspect Jesus did when he included them in the same sermon. Each requires a distinctly different approach to conflict, but they share the same goal—to replace human injustice with God's peace.

We must never give up the work of fighting for justice and the causes of righteousness. Sadly, many people in our nation and our world continue to experience abuse, mistreatment, racism, sexism, ageism, and other isms of discrimination and injustice. Because of the volatile fears and always-on-edge anxiety churning in so many of us today, we might be tempted to turn a blind eye, make a polite comment, or make a token donation. Whatever it takes to distance ourselves from the turmoil and potential trauma of calling out injustice and suffering the consequences. And I get it, because we cannot take every hill in every battle in every war raging around us.

But when we begin avoiding the fights we are called to fight, we lose a part of ourselves—our self-respect. We do not need to jump into every conflict, issue, or example of injustice. But we must be willing to know what causes matter most to us and which ones God has uniquely equipped and empowered us to fight.

And our goal when we do enter these battles must not be to win, to show others that we are right, that we are better people, or—heaven forbid—better Christians than they are. Our goal must be to bring God's peace to the places of strife and struggles for a bet-ter world. Keeping in mind that peace is not the absence of conflict, but the absence of an attitude of conflict, we shift the dynamics and flip the vibe among the contentious crowds around us.

Nowhere is this more challenging, I suspect, than with members of our own families. In our fractious and fragmented world today, most of us have experienced encounters with loved ones when we strongly, passionately disagree on important issues. It might be related to politics and government policies, to social issues and systemic attitudes, to personal decisions about lifestyles. If these heated exchanges don't happen in person, then they play out on social media with hurtful comments or ghosted silence.

Please allow me to suggest a different way of approaching these kinds of conflicts and emotionally charged conversations in which there is seemingly no middle ground. We've all been told to simply "agree to disagree," but I encourage you to flip it and "disagree to agree." What do I mean by this? I simply encourage you to acknowledge your love and respect for one another, despite whatever enormous issues or polarized positions separate you, and thus refuse to trade barbs, debate, or desire to force your point of view. In other words, assume that others will not hold the same perspective that you hold when it comes to topics that tend to be especially emotionally charged, such as politics, social issues, and religious practices. Allow them to have their own point of view, whether it happens to be similar to your own or not, and choose to respect them regardless.

Here's why. First, as you have likely discovered, neither of you is going to change the other's mind by citing facts, opinions, articles from online, or your favorite news personality. Some family members have even cited Scripture to me at times in an attempt to authoritatively trump my position on whatever issue of contention had flared up between us. If you want to see a pastor tempted to grieve the Spirit, then just try to use God's Word against him!

Thankfully, I did not take the bait in that situation. Because I knew that exegesis and theology were not going to do anything but add more fuel to the fiery topic ignited between us. So I took a couple of deep breaths, said a silent prayer, and told my dear family member, "It's okay for us to disagree because I love you more than I love the thought of changing your mind or attempting to prove I'm right. Can we agree on that?" So we allowed ourselves to disagree on the immediate topic at hand and focused instead on the larger bond we could agree on.

Next time you're faced with conflict, disagree to agree.

NO STRINGS ATTACHED

Being *pure in heart* in the overstimulated, corruption-is-encouraged culture we live in may sound as impossible as achieving world peace. But being open, honest, truthful, and vulnerable keeps our faith alive and reflects God's goodness in ways more powerful than any political movement, policy perspective, health crisis, natural disaster, or outbreak of violence. Which is why the world needs this kind of tenderhearted authentic love more than ever.

Lazy love relies on a self-protective shield of self-absorption and wants to assume that change—especially change inside another's heart—is not possible. Skepticism and cynicism harden our arteries and cause our hearts to become callous. Why open ourselves up to the risk of being totally honest? Why face possible rejection, ridicule, or rancor by revealing our fears, weaknesses, and anxieties?

The reason, once again, is because it is the true nature of love—real love, the kind with God as our wellspring, not the stagnant swamp of lazy love. This is also the only reason why we are called to *accept persecution* as part of our struggle to love boldly. And by persecution, I mean an anticipation and acceptance that others will oppose you. Because our love is never tested, sharpened, and effective if we engage only with others who agree with us, who look like us, who act like us. In the same sermon in which Jesus presented the Beatitudes, He reminded us to love purely—or, as He put it, perfectly:

> If you love those who love you, what reward will you get? Are not even the tax collectors doing that? And if you greet only your own people, what are you doing more than others? Do not even pagans do that? Be perfect, therefore, as your heavenly Father is perfect. (Matthew 5:46–48)

Please understand that Christ's admonition to be perfect here, perfect as our heavenly Father is perfect, is not about being free of flaws, weaknesses, mistakes, and sinful choices. Perfect here might be better translated as "whole," ripened to full maturity. It's not a matter of always doing everything right but of moving forward in love.

God knows we will make mistakes; say harsh words to our spouse or our kids and wish we could take them back; lie to a close friend to avoid listening to their latest crisis; undermine a coworker to make ourselves look better. But being aware that those are less-than-loving choices and then choosing differently tomorrow—that's growth and maturity approaching wholeness.

This movement into wholeness is what growing in love is all about. And it can take place only in relationships, in communities, in families. Otherwise, it withers and the life-giving arteries harden until the muscle atrophies and dies. With God as the source of our love, though, we are securely attached in ways that liberate us to love with no strings attached. No games. No manipulation. No agenda.

This kind of love, the kind that keeps our hearts tender and made of flesh and not stone, has flavor and substance, depth and light. In fact, in concluding His famous Sermon on the Mount, Jesus made two more comparisons that remind us what love tastes like and looks like:

> You are the salt of the earth. But if the salt loses its saltiness, how can it be made salty again? It is no longer good for anything, except to be thrown out and trampled underfoot.
>
> You are the light of the world. A town built on a hill cannot be hidden. Neither do people light a lamp and put it under a bowl. Instead they put it on its stand, and it gives light to everyone in the house. In the same way, let your light shine before others, that they may see your good deeds and glorify your Father in heaven. (Matthew 5:13–16)

Storge love demonstrates how you feel in your tender heart. It takes risks and learns from mistakes. It's as spicy as Taco Tuesdays with your fam and as sweet as the birthday cake you make for your spouse. It demonstrates love through sacred touch that's relaxed and never exploitative. It exercises restraint at times and marches into battle at others. It fights the good fight and brings the peace. It shines a light into the darkness and breaks down barriers. Like the bonds of family and the affection we show for those we love most, this love holds us close. We can feel safe and secure without fear of harm.

Storge love empowers us to be vulnerable, to surrender our strongholds of pretense, position, and posturing. Confident and fulfilled by our divine source of agape, we relinquish the human tendency to hide our wounds, keep struggles secret from others, and deny our failures. We remain open to needing and wanting loving relationships with others, which involves our attitudes and our behaviors, but we rest confidently in the knowledge of God's love as our foremost source of security. We feel the pain, hurt, and grief of betrayals and breakups, of shared burdens and communal losses, while continuing to trust God and lean into His love.

CHAPTER 12

Honorable Mention

I'm not concerned with your liking or disliking me...All I ask is that you respect me as a human being.

—Jackie Robinson

Honorable mention no longer gets the respect it deserves. Perhaps it has been overused or misused as a way of consoling or compensating individuals and teams whose performance did not merit the top spots. If you are a lover of sports, you know that nobody plays for a tie. With a tie no one wins and no one loses. There's no thrill of victory or regret of defeat. There's just that ambivalence over not being able to outscore or outplay your opponent.

Being awarded honorable mention, at least in sports, seems to land the same way. On one hand it's better than being overlooked, ignored, or unrecognized for what you contributed to the competition and your team. On the other hand, though, honorable mention seems less-than-significant, an afterthought or conspicuous consolation. I've sat through many an awards banquet, both when playing basketball as well as with my children, and observed the mixed emotions shown on the faces of those recognized by an honorable mention.

While the precise origin of giving an honorable mention remains unknown, it seems to have developed as a military commendation in centuries past. If a particular soldier was not eligible, apparently due to age or experience, for a medal or title or traditional award, then their commanding officers would recognize their performance with an HM. While there was no tangible or lingering indication, an honorable mention carried both honor and respect. In a sense it was a kind of customized award based on context and courage. From this perspective, it reflects the essence of storge love. It was a tangible way to recognize and express the unique facet of storge known as honor.

Honor relies on expressing storge love. Once again, without storge we can go through the motions and pay lip service to those we feel obliged to honor. But such duplicity and hypocrisy usually reveal themselves in subtle ways, such as disguising criticism and dishonor as humor or joking. We say we appreciate and honor others while intentionally withholding ways we could show them honor. We "forget" holidays or birthdays and minimize our communication.

You might feel justified in withholding storge love and the honor it bestows on others, such as your parents or siblings or spouse, because of how they have injured, betrayed, or abused you. Only when you are anchored by agape love can you then irrationally and gracefully honor others by forgiving them and showing them mercy.

Keep in mind, too, that forgiveness and honor are choices, not emotions, and that they do not ignore, erase, or minimize the weight of the offense. You can honor someone while still being honest about how they have hurt you, failed you, and disrespected you.

Storge love, like the other forms, relies on God as its source and expression.

HONOR ROLE

While affection and familiarity play a big part in defining storge love, the contributions of honor and respect are just as important. Particularly in the volatile, often divisive social and political culture in which we live, people inevitably disagree. As I indicated in the last chapter, I believe allowing disagreement is important while finding an area of shared agreement.

Exercising honor and respect remains just as essential, particularly when dealing with conflicts, opposing views, and different priorities. Honor and respect are not the same, although they both express value, significance, and esteem. If we search for definitions of "honor," most indicate that this quality expresses deep admiration and appreciation for someone or something, usually because of their role, authority, position, or contribution to a larger group. "Respect," by distinction, acknowledges excellence, often for achievement or character, based on performance.

Although there is some overlap between honor and respect, I consider honor to be based on the role, power, or leadership of someone. The fifth of the Ten Commandments tells us, "Honor your father and your mother, so that you may live long in the land the LORD your God is giving you" (Exod. 20:12). It carries a sense of paying homage and showing appreciation for our parents simply by the virtue of their being our parents. People have asked me, though, "Pastor, do I have to honor my parents if they don't deserve it?" This question typically comes from someone who experienced abuse, neglect, or harm from their parents.

My response reflects how honor differs from respect: "You honor that they gave you life without honoring how they failed to fulfill that role as your mother or father. You give them honorable mention without overlooking how they failed you." To support this distinction, I often cite, "[Parents,] do not provoke your children to anger by the way you treat them. Rather, bring them up with the discipline and instruction that comes from the Lord" (Eph. 6:4 NLT).

In other words, our parents are commanded to fulfill their roles as mothers and fathers honorably and to respect their children's roles as students and learners of the Lord, His Word, and His creation. Parents demonstrate the love of God and reflect His character to their children and the generations that follow. When parents obey God's Word, it's easier to honor them for the example they set because we benefit from their faithfulness and are blessed by their obedience.

On the other hand, when parents fail to follow God's guidelines and selfishly go their own route, then their choices directly and adversely affect their sons and daughters. First, we must understand and heed the warnings in Scripture regarding the responsibility of parents and their impact on future generations. The verse cited above from Ephesians may sound mild compared to some parental-impact verses from the Old Testament in which generational curses are described.

After Moses received the Ten Commandments from God and chiseled them into two stone tablets, the Lord passed before Moses and proclaimed, "The LORD, the LORD, the compassionate and gracious God, slow to anger, abounding in love and faithfulness, maintaining love to thousands, and forgiving wickedness, rebellion and sin. Yet he does not leave the guilty unpunished; he punishes the children and their children for the sin of the parents to the third and fourth generation" (Exod. 34:6–7). Other passages in the Old Testament make similar observations (see Exod. 20:5; Num. 14:18; Deut. 5:9) about the generational impact, often labeled "curses," of parental sin.

Some people interpret these verses as being clear absolutes about cause and effect, that when a person sins their children, grandchildren, great-grandchildren, and great-great-grandchildren will automatically suffer as well as part of their punishment. If we had only the ancient Hebrew Scriptures as God's Word, then I might concur. But the New Testament makes it abundantly clear again and again that Jesus changes everything—especially the old law under which the people of Israel had been living.

HONOR IS A PRIVILEGE

Once Jesus came, the way human beings relate to God the Father changed. Through the power of His death on the cross and the victory of the resurrection, Christ fulfilled the Law and gave us direct access to our heavenly Father through the power of the Holy Spirit. We're told, "Christ redeemed us from the curse of the law by becoming a curse for us, for it is written: 'Cursed is everyone who is hung on a pole.' He redeemed us in order that the blessing given to Abraham might come to the Gentiles through Christ Jesus, so that by faith we might receive the promise of the Spirit" (Gal. 3:13–14).

Please understand that we still often suffer as the result of our parents' sinful choices—but we are not doomed to live as cursed individuals being irrefutably punished. If our parents worshiped the idol of money or lived addicted to substances, if they allowed their own needs to always take priority over their children's needs, then those consequences shape how those children mature and the kind of adults (and parents) they become.

We see this impact transmitted across generations by the way we attach, or struggle to attach, to our parents based on their awareness and ability to provide security, love, safety, and comfort to us as children. The less our parents were able to be engaged with us and provide the attention, affirmation, and affection we all crave as fundamental, God-given needs, the more likely we suffer their failures.

But as we've already touched upon, we are not off the hook because our parents failed to love us perfectly. As we mature into adulthood, we assume responsibility for our own needs, our own decisions, our own actions. Yes, we are prone to be just as selfish and sinful as our parents unless—and this is huge—unless we embrace responsibility for the kind of man or woman we are becoming by surrendering our struggles and learn to rely on God and the body of Christ. Which comes back to the source of our love—fresh, limitless agape love? Or our own limited, stagnant supply?

When we experience the power of Jesus in our lives and walk by faith, then we break the chains of past generational bondage. Granted, the consequences and impact may linger, but any power the sins of our parents and ancestors hold over us is vanquished. We experience freedom, discover healing, and explore the purpose for which God created us. God's agape love infuses all areas and aspects of our lives.

Agape love also empowers us to show storge love by the way we honor and respect others, particularly our parents. But even if our parents failed us, hurt us, and neglected us in terrible ways, we cannot blame them for all of our choices, struggles, and regrets. We are new creatures in Christ and more than conquerors. We do not have to make the same mistakes our fathers made. We do not have to become who our mothers tried to make us be. We have autonomy within the Spirit to put God first and rely on His love.

As we experience spiritual transformation, we learn that giving and receiving honor is a privilege based on roles and positions. We can honor the basic blessings we received from our parents, however many or few those may be, and then make our own choices about whether we respect them. Because respect is earned through relationships that demonstrate the love of God both ways. Respect is the natural by-product of loving our neighbors as ourselves.

While honor may reside in the role, office, or position someone holds, respect is earned by how someone carries out their authority, responsibilities, and servant-leadership. Respect is about recognizing how one leads; honor is about acknowledging that one is a leader. Others might disagree or emphasize different nuances and language semantics. But as I consider storge love and its practice toward those for whom we hold affection and special regard, honor and respect need to be viewed as separate expressions.

We're called to honor those whose positions in our lives bless us in some way.

We're called to respect those whose integrity merits our acknowledgment of them.

CHALLENGING YET RESPECTING

Another important distinction is that honor carries more weight than respect. Even if we do not honor the person in a particular role or position of leadership, we can still honor the role. We may not like our boss, but we know we're called to honor his authority over us in the workplace. We may not like an individual leader in our community, state, or nation, but we choose to honor the office of mayor, governor, senator, or president. And, of course, this is far from easy when those wielding positions of power and authority abuse their privileges.

Yet how we choose to honor the position often earns the respect of those around us. How we choose to value parents, bosses, and leaders shows our willingness to hold tension in pursuit of overcoming lazy love. It's undeniably easier to dishonor others by letting our love get lazy.

When lazy love is our default setting, we refuse to disagree, to speak up, to ask because we fear the consequences. Lazy love will talk behind the back of your pastor, your supervisor, or your mayor, but tends to tell them what's expedient and conciliatory to their face. It acts the same way with family members and others in your tribe. Lazy love manipulates and schemes, second-guesses and self-serves. Lazy love is one of the most insidious ways to undermine those we are called to love, the ones we feel forced to honor but struggle to respect.

Once we dishonor authority, then we disrespect all leaders and believe ourselves exempt from obedience. We undermine their leadership in subtle—and not so subtle—ways. This might take the form of rumor and gossip or outright assassination of another's character. It might be an ambiguous email, ghosted text, or anonymous comment on social media.

Respect accrues and builds a legacy, which means it can also crumble and deteriorate if someone betrays you, breaches their integrity in relating to you, or harms you. People lose our respect when they fail to be consistent with the caring, Christlike person they've been previously; when they begin taking shortcuts, climbing ladders at the expense of relationships, and leading by ego and not agape.

Respect requires courageous love, a willingness to honor those in authority without overlooking their blind spots or ignoring injustices. This balance of acknowledging imperfection while still respecting and honoring can be tricky, but it's what storge love requires. It bears the tension of loving a flawed human being who plays an important role in your life. And storge love deepens the love and affection within those relationships.

DELEGATION AND DEFERENCE

Storge love tends to be anchored by affection, familiarity, and acceptance. In addition to our family members, it's what we often experience with our neighbors, our coworkers, and members of our small group or Bible study at church. These relationships typically form based on proximity and circumstances, shared interests, or similar values. Just as you did not get to choose the particular family into which you were born, storge-based relationships usually rely on intersecting lives rather than deliberate choices.

While you choose where you live and the kind of home you inhabit, you generally don't get to choose your neighbors. Now many people base their choice of locale on the kinds of people they observe or perceive to be their neighbors, often to reinforce that they themselves are the same kind of person. For example, you want a nice, well-kept home in a safe, upscale neighborhood so based on appearances, you assume that residents there are like-minded. They, too, are pleasant, community-minded, security-conscious individuals pursuing excellence in their lives. But this doesn't guarantee that you will like, accept, or enjoy one another.

Similarly, workplaces can be some of the most challenging contexts for displaying storge love through honor and respect. Because at work most of us are forced to collaborate, cooperate, and cocreate with individuals we don't necessarily get to choose. We're hired into a business and assigned to an already existing department with team members already in place. Rather than rush in to impress others, establish our superior skills, and demonstrate our ambition, storge love compels us to come alongside, to observe before offering feedback, to learn from others instead of covering our insecurities through swagger.

Two of the key aspects of showing storge love at work are *delegation* and *deference*. Neither of these is new, but from what I've experienced and observed, they are both underutilized. Delegation tends to be something elusive that every micromanager and controlling leader intends to do or promises to do but seldom does, at least not for long. Rather than show respect for others' capabilities and skills, lazy-love leaders refuse to let go or insist on systems operating their way and no other.

Servant leaders, however, trust God with outcomes and know He has placed them within groups, teams, and organizations to be part of something, not all of something. With faith as their foundation, they are released to love others by trusting them to do a good job—even if they do it differently from the way others have done it. They're free to love others by helping them succeed rather than viewing others' talents and abilities as a threat to their own competence.

Faith-fueled team members are also willing to defer to one another's unique contribution. Every team decision does not have to be a debate with a winner and a loser. Instead, such directions emerge out of shared ideas that come together to look at all angles before setting course. Deference gets a bad rep because it may feel like passivity, like giving up and giving in, refusing to engage in order to let others do their thing.

Like meekness and humility, showing deference simply means putting others first—or at least right next to you! Deference is a way to show honor and respect for what and how others contribute. One of my favorite examples goes back to college and a particular friend who often invited me to stay and eat with his family at mealtimes. While there was no formality, I liked the way they did things, setting the table and then not allowing anyone to begin eating until those who prepared the meal were seated and served first. Another example is being consistent with punctuality. If you're always running behind, then don't complain if others are as well. If you're on time, then consider how you can help those around you align to the same rhythm.

BRIDGE TO EROS

Storge love, at least in my thinking, also provides the perfect bridge into our final form of divine love—eros. While we will explore eros in depth in the next section, let's consider the way storge's components of affection, honor, and respect provide a crucial framework upon which eros builds its home. You'll recall that all of these forms of love overlap and interconnect, and this is certainly the case with storge and eros.

You would think that affection between a husband and a wife would be a given, but I know this is not necessarily the case. Several men over the years have confided to me that something troubles them in their marriages. Their wives loved them, valued them, trusted them, and cherished them—and yet, these husbands struggled to know if their wives *enjoyed* them. The primary evidence for them was lack of affection. Not lack of sexual intercourse and lovemaking—but lack of affection.

"I know my wife loves me, but I'm not sure she likes me," one brother confided. He went on to acknowledge that their relational styles differed based on wildly contrasting family dynamics for each while growing up. His wife's family was more reserved, not very demonstrative, and comfortable without the hugs and touch that he had known as a kid. When he had asked her if she was willing to be more affectionate with him, she agreed and yet struggled to follow through. Consequently, he felt like he was too needy and tended to withdraw or not ask her to show affection.

I emphasized to him that affection is not merely our willingness to touch or hug another person. Affection is our heart's attitude toward them. Storge love enjoys serving and anticipating the needs of others, and our spouse deserves this kind of singular attention from us like no one else in our lives. We should never have to doubt how special we are to the one committed to loving us as our husband or wife.

Similarly, we must also practice showing respect and honor to our spouses—in the ways that matter to them! Just as we're familiar with learning one another's love languages, we must also discover and speak our partner's language of storge love. What makes them feel honored? What reminds them that you respect them—as a man or a woman, as a dad or a mom, as a friend, as a follower of Jesus?

Simply put, the best way we can honor and respect our spouse is by putting them first and being their number one fanboy or fangirl. Putting them first does not mean ignoring your own needs or playing the martyr. Putting them first means making sure you're in a strong, centered place from which to serve them. Putting them first does not mean you are putting yourself last. Which is why meeting one another's needs must be a foundational priority in marriage.

Being your mate's number one fan may sound corny or insincere, but you would be surprised what a difference it makes to have a cheerleader who sees you and is always there believing in you and urging you on. My wife and I were with another couple not long ago, and the husband joked about how his wife rarely compliments him on anything. The wife half-jokingly said, "Well, I don't want him to get the big head and think he's all that! He might not need me anymore!" My wife and I exchanged one of those glances that communicate quite a lot without saying anything but decided not to comment in that moment.

Later, after we were alone, my wife said, "I *do* want you to get a big head! Because I know how great you really are! And I'm secure enough to know you know how great I am, too!" Storge love not only knows how great our spouse is but looks for opportunities to show more than tell them. How? By attending events that you know are important to him. By praising all the ways she makes your home a beautiful place.

Honor and respect in marriage take storge love to another level. Which is what eros is all about—so let's get started!

THREAT #4

Confusing Sex with Intimacy due to Lack of Eros

"Haven't you read," he replied, "that at the beginning the Creator 'made them male and female,' and said, 'For this reason a man will leave his father and mother and be united to his wife, and the two will become one flesh'? So they are no longer two, but one flesh. Therefore what God has joined together, let no one separate."

MATTHEW 19:4-6

Better to be miserable with her than happy without her. Let our hearts break provided they break together. If the voice within us does not say this it is not the voice of Eros.

C. S. LEWIS

CHAPTER 13

Lazy Lust

Lust is the craving for salt of a man who is dying of thirst.
—Frederick Buechner

Imagine you're traveling and find yourself in an unfamiliar city, a large urban environment where no one knows you. Ahead of your arrival, though, you have conducted online searches to help you find what you're looking for. You have an address in a run-down neighborhood housing the destination you've been anticipating for a long time. While a sense of guilt and shame attempt to impede your journey there, your excitement continues to grow. Furtively glancing around to see if anyone is watching, you discreetly go through the doorway and pay the entrance fee.

Taking your seat in the large dimly lit theater, you can barely make out the silhouettes of the others seated all around you. The curtained stage draws your gaze, and you can't wait to see what's about to be revealed. A familiar scent begins to waft through the air, which only heightens your anticipation and teases your senses.

Finally, the auditorium lights fade into darkness. Upbeat instrumental jazz begins as the curtains slowly part. Your heart drums faster as you stare into the spotlight. Then, ever so slowly, the domed silver cover rises from the enormous platter, revealing what you've all come there to see: a heap of sizzling maple-glazed bacon, a perfectly cooked slab of Wagyu beef, mounds of garlic mashed potatoes, and a tower of bright strawberries delicately coated in wet dark chocolate. Everyone rises to their feet, cheering and clapping, yelling for more.

Sounds silly, doesn't it?

Why would adults pay to gather in a clandestine location just to look at food?

This imaginary scenario illustrates the point that author and theologian C. S. Lewis famously made about lust. In such a place where people would gather to be titillated by what they wanted to taste, "would you not think that... something had gone wrong with the appetite for food?"[1]

We mistakenly assume lust is only about sex.

But lust is about a human appetite, specifically a craving for more.

A craving that cannot be filled except by love.

When you confuse sex with intimacy, you set yourself up for lazy love.

AS LAZY AS IT GETS

Lust is as lazy as love gets.

You only have to think about the appeal of pornography for a moment to see this illustrated. It relies on observing, imagining, and distancing yourself while pretending to participate. It requires none of the risk involved in loving someone. There's no fear of rejection or abandonment. You can return and view it from the safety and privacy of your home as many times as you want. There's no emotional vulnerability in sharing your fears and dreams, your secrets and suffering. And there's no intimacy, no connection with another human being.

With lust, there's only detachment, dehumanization, and destabilization. If lazy love prevents us from loving fully the way God intends, then lust takes lazy to a whole new level. Lazy love often attempts to relate to others, albeit in mostly passive and selfish ways. Lazy lust focuses only on pleasure within itself, excluding relationships except as ingredients expedient to obtaining personal fulfillment.

Most people tend to think of lust primarily as a physical problem, usually involving sexual urges and desires gone astray outside of marriage. While that's certainly one dimension of lust, its insatiable appetite extends into virtually every area of our lives. Because at its essence, lust relies on idolatry. Jesus said, "For where your treasure is, there your heart will be also" (Matt. 6:21). Lust promises to provide a treasure map to whatever you're craving at your deepest levels of longing. If you pursue its treasure, then you can experience whatever you lack and desire.

Lust tells you there's something you can do, eat, drink, buy, own, and enjoy that will fulfill you unlike anything else. Lust says that you don't need anyone else—it can satisfy you. Lust is often the appetite of addiction, the hunger and thirst within for something to take away your pain, your loneliness, your emptiness, your loss and disappointment with life. God's Word makes a clear distinction between the source of lust and the source of love: "For everything in the world—the lust of the flesh, the lust of the eyes, and the pride of life—comes not from the Father but from the world. The world and its desires pass away, but whoever does the will of God lives forever" (1 John 2:16–17).

The lust of the flesh, the lust of the eyes, and the pride of life all originate from the world. The wellspring of agape love spilling over into all other loves comes from God. Lust is horizontal and refuses to look up, to look beyond where it stands. Love is not only vertical but all-consuming. We cannot be separated from God's love, but we can step away from the lusts of the world. You can't change love, but love can—and will—change you. So as we begin considering how to overcome the power of lust to numb our capacity for love, I encourage you to consider what and whom your heart treasures right now.

And ask yourself, Is it *love*... or is it *lust?*

WHEN EROS GOES ASTRAY

Perhaps the best-known of our four loves, eros includes the passionate, romantic, and sexual expressions of love between two people wanting to consummate desire, fulfill attraction, and connect without shame. Eros encompasses the power of desire and attraction, the union of a man and a woman, becoming one as God intended when He recognized it was not good for Adam to be alone in the garden and so He created Eve (see Gen. 2:18). But eros also encompasses so much more than the physical acts of procreative lovemaking.

Eros is ultimately about intimacy.

Eros is about being known.

Lust is all about hiding.

Lust camouflages sex as intimacy while undermining the possibility for real connection.

And plenty of people choose to hide in the darkness of lust when it comes to longing for eros. And, yes, this darkness often attempts to hijack and eclipse our sexuality. Numerous men approach me as their pastor for prayer, for healing, sometimes just for truth-sharing about the battles with lust they're facing and feel too ashamed to confess to anyone else. Early in my ministry, most of them were younger, having grown up with early exposure to online porn. Now, after ministering for more than twenty years, the men who confide in me represent a spectrum of ages, stages, and wages. Of course I understand that women face this same battle, although it might have different nuances. Human lust is basically eros gone astray, derailed from its target of true intimacy.

Regardless of how their struggles may differ, they share the common denominator of exceeding the boundaries they know God has established for their own good. No matter what their individual manifestations may look like, they all know the way lust can temporarily seem to win the tug-of-war with love.

Ultimately, this is the power struggle composing any battle with lust. Because it undermines love, lust attempts to cast a spell of powerful self-deception. When you've tasted authentic love, however, both divine and human, you eventually get sick of what lust continues to serve. Because lust pulls you away from the intimacy you crave while trying to convince you that you don't need it or can get it without risking vulnerability with relationship to others. Lust tries to convince you that sex or whatever you're craving can be separated from the rest of you, compartmentalized and compressed away from your heart and soul.

Such objectification ultimately takes a toll, though, and we become fragmented from the fullness of our humanity, from the sacred qualities instilled by God in us, and from the longing to attach securely and enjoy the safety of a committed relationship with our spouse. Consequently, lust will always leave a bad taste in your spirit.

Like fast food, lust exploits our hunger for the love we're lacking only to leave us feeling lonely, empty, and nauseous with shame. As we try to get the love we need, however, we often give in to lust rather than face past losses and the risks of loving again. If we want to experience the overflowing abundance of love that God designed us to enjoy, including its physical expression grounded in eros, then we must recognize the cycles we keep repeating. We must realize when we choose lust as a default, then defuse the derailment of intimacy and realign with true eros in order to love in divine synchronicity.

SPIRITUAL INTIMACY

Lust never satisfies because it defies how God made us to crave relationship and to long for intimacy. It's been this way from the beginning of humankind. While God could have allowed Adam to exist independently, in relationship with only God, the Creator wanted Adam to know intimacy and communion and connection with another human, someone like him yet distinctly different. Both male and female reflect God's divine image and together form a complementary glimpse of who He is. Both contain overlapping as well as distinct godly qualities and image imprints. When male and female come together, they reflect a fuller picture of the One who made them, a clearer illustration of how Christ relates to the church.

This union is the spiritual essence of eros.

In addition to providing union and connection, eros love also reflects dimensions of the other three kinds of love. The friendship and enjoyable companionship of phileo love is present, along with the honor and respect of storge love. And, of course, eros originates in the divine selflessness and generative creativity of agape love, literally the act of making love by becoming one flesh.

While the Bible contains numerous examples, we see this abundantly in the Song of Songs in the Old Testament, the poetry of divine love in which two lovers express in words and images their passionate desire for intimacy. Notice right from the beginning the sensuality and poetic beauty of this dialogue:

> Let him kiss me with the kisses of his mouth—
>> for your love is more delightful than wine.
> Pleasing is the fragrance of your perfumes;
>> your name is like perfume poured out.
> No wonder the young women love you!
> Take me away with you—let us hurry!
> Let the king bring me into his chambers. (Song of
> Songs 1:2–4)

Pretty steamy, right? But also wholesome and without shame or gratuitous eroticism. This is God's Word to His people, and this entire book shows us the sacred beauty and spiritual depth in eros love. The descriptive metaphors are especially apt and appeal to the senses, including not just sight but taste and smell. "Your love is more delightful than wine" and "your name is like perfume poured out" both evoke sensory power and celebrate those pleasurable sensations. Wine and perfume would have been part of a Jewish marriage celebration and convey the same sense of celebration today.

The beauty and sensuality we find in Solomon's Song of Songs seem a far cry from the ubiquity of sex, eroticism, and pornography in our culture today. Sexuality in all its forms has become a consumer commodity rather than a deeply personal gift to be shared within its intended unveiling. This objectification of our sexuality ultimately takes a toll, though, and we become fragmented from the fullness of our humanity, from the sacred qualities instilled by God in our sexuality, and from the longing to attach securely and enjoy the safety of a committed relationship with our spouse.

LUST LIVES ON LIES

Part of our problem with lust stems from the narrow focus on our sexuality. But to understand its power, we must realize the greater appetite and intense desire from which lust emerges. While we may understand and experience lust in our sexual desires, we must look further to identify it as a passionate, overwhelming desire or craving for something to provide fulfillment, purpose, and satisfaction in our lives. We may know intellectually that God is the only One who can fill that deep hunger within us, but that doesn't prevent us from seeking out idols for a temporary fix.

Lust results in a convergence of spiritual, emotional, and psychological longings that seek expression in consumption. Often lust exploits opportunities when our longing for more in life intersects with our body's reaction to pleasure, comfort, and escape from pain. This is the recipe for counterfeit intimacy. We want more—more connection, more security, more affirmation and affection, more pleasure—and nothing the world offers satisfies us for very long.

This desire for more reflects our deepest desire as well as our greatest fear—to be known. So often I hear lessons on sexual purity and healthy intimacy focused only on the consequences of lust described by Paul in his epistles collected in the New Testament. But the problem with lust is basic to our humanity from the beginning of creation. Back in the garden of Eden, Eve and Adam gave in to a lust for the fruit they were told was off-limits, the fruit that the serpent cunningly used as a pivot point for their disobedience against God.

The first man and woman knew that God had placed parameters around the fruit from a certain tree, and yet rather than trust God, they entertained the question the enemy used to ignite their curiosity and desire: "Did God really say, 'You must not eat from any tree in the garden'?" (Gen. 3:1). Questioning what you know to be true often leads to separation—from God, from yourself, and from your true longings.

When Eve answers that God had indeed forbidden them from eating fruit from one particular tree, the serpent outright lies both about the consequences and about who God is: "You will not certainly die... For God knows that when you eat from it your eyes will be opened, and you will be like God, knowing good and evil" (Gen. 3:4–5). Lust whispers that you are the exception, that the same rules do not apply to you. Lust convinces you to believe that somehow you can be satisfied and unscathed by the consequences of this deception.

These lies of lust are the same ones the enemy feeds us today when we're tempted to yield to our appetites in hopes of finding fulfillment from any of our idols. He tells us that there will be no destructive consequences, that there's really no harm in tasting forbidden fruit. We tell ourselves that no one will be harmed if we entertain that little fantasy in our minds about our attractive coworker. We choose to believe that we're the exception to God's guidelines and won't become addicted to looking at certain images online. We deny that our marriage suffers when we pour ourselves into career advancement rather than relationship enhancement. We pretend that focusing on our image and appearance at the expense of our relationships has nothing to do with lust.

The enemy also tries to convince us that God's holding out on us, preventing us from enjoying what's meant to be enjoyed. This is the ultimate FOMO, the fear of missing out on something that can make us feel better, more beautiful, more powerful, more secure, more comforted, more affirmed. Lust can use anything we're not getting in our real lives as bait for our imaginations and temptations. Things are different now than they were in biblical times, we tell ourselves. We persuade ourselves that our needs can be met differently today than in ancient times.

But if we've experienced love, then we know these lies can never be true. We can tell ourselves these falsehoods as frequently as we like, but the truth is that our heart's own dissatisfaction will eventually force us to see self-deception for what it is. Lust tells you that it's okay to have something that God has placed outside the boundaries for you. And it's not that love exists only within God's boundaries—love is God's boundary around you. When you step outside of being grounded in God's love, then lazy love becomes lust before your very eyes.

SHAME ON YOU

By this point I hope you agree that lust is a problem extending beyond your sexuality, one that affects you both directly and indirectly in your capacity to love—yourself, God, and others. So how can you overcome it? How can you remain grounded in love rather than uprooted by lust?

I'm convinced one of the most effective tools in recognizing lust is identifying shame. I'm not talking about guilt over certain actions or having convictions within your conscience, which are often prompted by God's Spirit. No, shame may be the most powerful lie that the enemy uses against us. Shame cuts to the heart of who we are as image-bearers of God. Shame tells us we're not worthy, not valuable, not seen or noticed, not accepted, and not loved. Shame wants us to believe that we are the problem, that no one can know all the secrets inside us without judging and rejecting us.

After Adam and Eve swallowed the bitter fruit of the serpent's lies, they became aware of a new reality—basically an awareness of what they lost by disobeying God. The perfect connection to God and to one another gets severed—not irreparably but significantly. No longer do they know the security and safety, the intimate connection to their Holy Creator and to each other as His complementary image-bearers.

Instead, shame wedges itself into their lives. They go from the freedom of innocence they knew in the garden—"Adam and his wife were both naked, and they felt no shame" (Gen. 2:25)—to an emotional hangover of epic proportions—"Then the eyes of both of them were opened, and they realized they were naked" (Gen. 3:7). They pivot from naked-and-no-shame to naked-where's-my-fig-leaf. Shame saturates us with an unbearable sense of self-loathing, one that's often so painful we look for escape and comfort—driving us into an addictive cycle with whatever we idolize.

Shame fuels lust just as being known facilitates love. And the key to dispelling shame and pursuing true intimacy—with God and with others—is living in the fullness of truth. When truth is our foundation, we can build relationships that enable trust and vulnerability to emerge. With them as pillars, we discover the joy of intimacy, which I'm convinced is the heart of eros love. Intimacy is reflected in our ability to be naked and unashamed with another person, but being naked with someone never guarantees intimacy with them.

True intimacy touches that longing for more, for the divine, for the union of all you are with all God has made someone else to be. There's freedom and confidence in how you relate, an interdependence that is neither codependent nor individuated. You become more and more vulnerable, removing layers of fig leaves you've been hiding behind, sometimes for your entire life. You strip away the lies, the self-deceptions, and discover yourself reflected in the love of another, through the love of God.

WHERE EROS AND AGAPE MEET

If you want to overcome lazy love and dispel the power of lust to derail your ability to love, then live in the truth. Begin with yourself and God's Word. Learn who He says you are and what you share in common with other human beings. See yourself as the beloved child of the King you are. Recognize your worth as His son or daughter who is loved unconditionally—no matter what you've done or how long you've done it.

You will also need to face the truth about what's been lost. Adam and Eve had to come to terms with the consequences of their decisions to give in to the lust of their eyes. To deny what we've lost tends to empower our willingness to continue settling for lust rather than love. Practically speaking, facing our losses requires grieving and suffering, which we're often conditioned to avoid. Rather than acknowledging the loss of our marriage or a romantic relationship, we try to compensate by getting back in the game. We try to distract ourselves by thinking we need to find someone else or at least lose ourselves in some lustful, idolatrous pursuit.

The problem with lust, as we've seen, is that it's simply not sustainable. It can never satisfy, distract, or compensate us for long enough. Which forces us either to ramp up our lustful desires and pursuits or to confront the emptiness, fear, anger, and sadness inside us. To seek the presence of Jesus inside our pain. To confide in trusted family and phileo-friends who are willing to share our pain and to comfort us.

In this life we will inevitably experience breakups and lose boyfriends and girlfriends; some will even break engagements and call off weddings. About half of the population will experience a divorce from someone they once thought was their God-given partner for life. We face these losses not because the two parties are bad people, but because we as a society condition ourselves to look for others who can meet our needs.

As we've already seen, meeting one another's needs interdependently is healthy and necessary. But relying on someone else exclusively or predominantly holding them responsible for your needs won't sustain the relationship. When our needs change, then we often change the person we're in a relationship with. Lazy love insists on having its needs met the way it wants them met, and when that changes or shifts, then lazy love often decides to interview new potential partners.

Love, on the other hand, accepts change as part of the process of loving one another. Love says, "When you change, I change, too. We will not grow apart or go in different directions because we will continue to change and keep pace with one another." Love is fluid and dynamic and flows toward others, while lust is rigid, static, and self-centered. Love adapts and finds a way to not only sustain relationship but strengthen it. Lust remains uptight while love is always loose.

This is the relational model we witness in the three persons of God. For God so loved the world and wanted to ensure that none would perish that He became human in the form of His Son, Jesus. God the Son loved us so much that He suffered, died, and arose from the dead to defeat sin and death once and for all. When Jesus ascended into heaven after His resurrection, He sent the third member of the Godhead, the Holy Spirit, to dwell in His followers. God continually met His children where they are and still does today. If He had loved us less or lusted after having control of us, then He would not have changed. But in His wisdom, compassion, and power, He shared different facets of His character to meet our needs.

While even the best human relationships remain limited in their ability to satisfy our deepest longings, the love of God knows no bounds. His love is eternal and infuses our ability to love others with this timeless quality that transcends seasons, singleness, solitude, and separation. This is where eros and agape meet. This is where we discover intimacy in eros that leads us to spiritual connection and mature growth.

Eros love, sourced by your singular supply of agape, sees others with clarity, compassion, and care. When eros becomes untethered from agape, the result obscures your view of other people in the fullness of their beauty and humanity and looks through a lustful lens of objectified attributes and ignited arousal templates. When your eros lacks agape as its source, you easily confuse sex with intimacy, lust with acceptance and affirmation. This confusion blurs eros into merely the erotic.

Eros without agape usually defaults to lazy lust. There's surface attraction but not lasting satisfaction. The way to combat lust, whether the lust for sex or for money or for whatever idol appeals, is to allow eros to reflect agape. Because intimacy reflects the essence of God's love.

If you want to remove the threat posed by confusing sex for intimacy, then the generative power of eros holds the key.

CHAPTER 14

The Heartbeat of Eros

Don't ever think I fell for you or fell over you. I didn't fall in love, I rose in it.

—Toni Morrison

A woman steps forward and receives a single, long-stemmed red rose from a man.

She looks elegantly gorgeous in her formfitting gown, perfect makeup, and expertly styled hair. While she claims to be a nurse from Atlanta, her beautiful face and stunning eyes look like those of a model or an online influencer. Her hand trembles slightly holding her rose as tears form in her eyes. Her expression reflects just the right mix of surprise, humility, confidence, and subtle seduction.

The tuxedo-clad prince looks like someone you've seen before, a former pro athlete perhaps or the host of an outdoor lifestyle show. He's handsome in a boyish way that's balanced by a rugged edge of beard stubble and a steely smile. Agonizing for weeks over his final selection, he chose to give his final rose to the princess standing before him, the woman he says he wants to marry and spend the rest of his life with.

The camera moves closer, mesmerized by the way they stare into each other's eyes. They embrace and share a passionate kiss as onlookers cheer and clap while rose petals fall like confetti. Moments later they're whisked away in a private luxury SUV, presumably to the airport for some exotic vacation in the next chapter of their glamorous, utterly romantic lives.

I love the way reality romance shows often distill the essence of eros into distinct ingredients. Like the blend of essential oils and herbal notes to create an enticing new perfume, these programs appeal to our desire to be known and loved, to experience the fullness of life alongside our heart's companion. Everyone wants to know how to satisfy the longings of their heart for connection, that sense of fulfillment God had in mind when He created woman because it wasn't good for man to be alone (see Gen. 2:18).

The problem, however, is that we don't usually see what's behind the scenes of our favorite reality romances. We overlook how much work went into production, into editing, into music and special effects, into all the technical wizardry that contributes to a polished program. Relationships require hard work, and you must be willing to labor behind the scenes as well as in front of the eyes of those around you.

Focusing only on appearances, on sex appeal, never satisfies the soul.

YOU CAN'T DANCE TO ALGORITHMS

No doubt about it, eros has become a major pillar of television programming. And what we watch often reflects the ways dating, courtship, romance, and marriage have evolved in recent generations. What was true for the ways our parents and grandparents met and kindled their relationships may not be the same for us today.

Certain elements, however, remain timeless no matter how dramatically cultures change.

While dating may seem old-fashioned, romantic relationships remain timeless. Culture has historically influenced how we view relationships and the requisite etiquette and protocol for pursuing a spouse. With today's younger generations—say, millennials and those behind them—we see that many no longer want the encumbrance of commitment or the permanence of marriage. This doesn't mean that eros love is no longer relevant, only that cultural views on how two people share it varies.

In my parents' time, most people pursued marriage and then stayed together for their children, for social approval, and for lifestyle security. But what did staying together despite the lack of eros love communicate to their children and those around them? What picture of marriage emerged? Perhaps no wonder current trends shy away from an institution that seemed to limit more than unleash, to inhibit more than inspire, and to frustrate more than fulfill.

In many ways current views of romantic relationships reflect the prevailing culture of endless-option consumerism and technical totality. Recently my daughter and I were at Disney World, and when we returned to our hotel, we saw at least a half dozen lawn mowers, self-propelled and unmanned, cutting the emerald-green expanses enveloping the property. While it was both surreal and futuristic, this sight made me reflect on how artificial intelligence continues to change our lives.

And why should relationships be any different? With AI and all the dynamic fluidity it provides users, individuals don't have to make decisions and choose consequences anymore. When I was growing up, if you played video games, you had to get up, put the game cartridge into the player, make sure the cords were all connected and plugged in, and then sit back down and grab the control panel with its directional buttons and joystick. If we got tired of that game and wanted another, we had to get up and repeat the process.

When I play games with my kids now, we barely have to move our eyes and fingertips. Now they can play games with people on other continents without leaving the couch. They can switch games, play multiple games, purchase new ones—all with the swipe of a screen or the press of a button.

Automated cars continue to assume more control over driving functions. Learning how to drive, I had to be sure to look in my side mirrors and rearview mirror, remaining alert to sudden shifts in traffic or unexpected obstacles. Now, the electronic intel of the vehicle does all this and so much more. Drivers become more like passengers, controlling with commands much like playing a video game.

Relationships have become similar in some ways. People don't have to commit because they have options and can let social media and AI do the work of selecting potential partners for them. Algorithms and apps can make selections, arrange times and places to meet, reserve tables, place orders, and pay tabs. If things don't work out, you can block the person and delete them from your contacts.

Despite such remarkable conveniences, though, you still need human engagement with the variables that impact your growth, maturity, and contentment. No app can fix broken hearts and no website can heal your trauma. You can't slow dance to algorithms! You have to do some things yourself, and in order to understand the purpose in your power to choose, you need divine guidance. You need to know yourself well enough to enjoy being alone with yourself—and with God.

REALITY CHECK

The other challenge presented by technology is the way people would rather watch others experience romantic relationships than risk them personally. Just as the online accessibility of pornographic content exploits lust through erotica, the cultural narrative exploits romance and the emotional longings it ignites. Romantic eros, when experienced vicariously as a viewer, rents out the longing in our hearts for deep connection and intimacy. We can watch others fall in love and feel happy for them without risking any part of our own hearts. We don't have to feel pressure to look our best let alone share vulnerably. We can be romance voyeurs.

Getting our romance fix from watching others also alleviates some of the pressure to find a partner. Despite our progressive shifts in how we meet and date, the cultural pressure to be part of a couple remains. If you're single, the pressure to find someone can be overwhelming. Even within the church—some would say, *especially* within the church—the emphasis on marriage can make singles feel incomplete, lacking, and insufficient. Like their lives are not fulfilling unless they have a spouse, children or plans for some, and a beautiful home to provide shelter for this domestic dream. While this social pressure sounds old-fashioned and outdated, it lingers like a phantom limb, reminding you of what you don't have even if that's not what you actually want.

The solution to being single is to realize that it does not require a solution! Singleness is not a problem to be solved, a rehearsal for when you finally meet a mate, or a punishment for whatever relational mistakes you may have made. Singleness is simply part of our lives that varies in duration from season to season and person to person. It is a gift as much as marriage is a gift. With this understanding as a baseline, then, the unique gifts of being single should be embraced and savored.

Two relationships in our lives remain inescapable—our relationship with God and our relationship with ourselves. Singleness affords unique opportunities to focus on each of these relationships.

SHOWING UP FOR YOURSELF

When it comes to love, you might not consider singleness essential to understanding eros. But it is. Without knowing who you are, what you need, and what you have to offer, you will never discover how to relate to a romantic partner in ways that explore the union eros offers for a man and a woman. In order to experience that oneness, the kind God described as "leaving and cleaving" (see Gen. 2:24 KJV; Matt. 19:5), you have to be able to hold the tension between being an individual and a couple at the same time.

If you remain too individuated, then you will never know the rest, security, trust, and soul connection that come from knowing another. If you abandon yourself to become one with another, you risk unhealthy codependency. Both ends of this relational spectrum require knowing yourself and your needs independently before you ever consider choosing to enter into an interdependence with anyone else.

The problem with knowing yourself is, of course, our old friend lazy love. When coupled with painful circumstances, unmet needs from childhood, and a solid anchoring in agape love, you set yourself up to reinforce your attachment style when relating with others. You long for relationship but remain too committed to protecting and defending yourself from getting hurt, rejected, and abandoned. Or, you long for relationship so desperately that you cannot endure the pain of being alone with your losses, needs, and insecurities.

Until you can sustain and nurture being alone with yourself, however, you will never find your center and discover true intimacy with God. Regardless of whether we're married or single, we automatically associate our aloneness with being lonely. As you'll recall, the two are not the same and are not synonymous. You can be alone and not lonely just as easily as you can be lonely and not alone. The pivot point in each case is how you relate to yourself.

We tend to view loneliness as a painful condition that requires connection to alleviate. While this is true, we're prone to overlook the fact that we can always show up for ourselves, befriend ourselves, and be present with ourselves no matter what else is going on in our lives. Depending on our personalities and past histories, we may squirm at the thought of being alone with ourselves because of all the thoughts and feelings that emerge. Without other people, events, and circumstances to distract us, we're forced to come to terms with painful realities we've likely been avoiding.

I'm reminded of a younger man I'm mentoring who recently shared something his counselor observed. In his mid-twenties, this man is in recovery for drugs and alcohol and coming up on a year of sobriety in his journey. One of his struggles emotionally stems from feeling lonely, that sense of not being connected to others who get him and accept him. His loneliness feels so powerful at times that he doesn't know how to avoid being consumed by it.

He knows there are people in our church, including myself and my wife, who believe in him and are there for him. But those feelings of being alone and on his own have been with him for as long as he can remember. He knows that he learned to escape himself by relying on other substances to alter his mood and mindset. Now that he's sober and committed to his recovery, he accepts that he has to learn to face his loneliness.

Thankfully, he's discovering that when he shows up for himself, his loneliness loses its power over him and its pain seems much milder. One day we met for coffee and he had just come from therapy with his counselor. When he told his therapist how lonely he felt, the counselor paused and then observed, "You're not lonely. You're just not sure how to be present with yourself—especially when you're in pain." My friend knew his therapist was right—and I suspect this observation holds true for many of us.

Do you know how to be present with yourself?

Could it be that you're not lonely but unskilled in showing up for yourself?

LOVE YOURSELF AS YOUR NEIGHBOR

Learning how to show up for yourself means more than becoming the person you want to date. While that is excellent advice for moving forward and self-improving, you need to do more than that. You need to become the person who knows how to enjoy being with yourself. You need to treat yourself the way you want others to treat you.

When Jesus reminds us to "love your neighbor as yourself" (Matt. 22:39; Mark 12:31), He implies that we inherently know how to love ourselves in a way that's consistent with how we want to be treated. Sometimes I wonder, though, if we need reminding to "love yourself as you love your neighbor." Because I don't want to be loved the same way I sometimes see others failing to love themselves!

I suspect you know many people, just as I do, who appear to treat others with kindness, respect, compassion, grace, hospitality, and generosity—but fail to extend these same gifts to themselves.

The dissonance between their treatment of others and their treatment of themselves might manifest as self-deprecation, a sense of
"You deserve what I'm giving you so much more than I do." This,
in fact, may be an attempt to love themselves vicariously by means
of what psychologists call transference. Self-deprecators cannot
directly show kindness to themselves but they can receive a sense of
it by giving it to others.

Another manifestation of this disconnect between loving yourself and loving others is martyrdom. I don't mean this literally but
figuratively because of the way some people continually give, serve,
volunteer, lead, provide, and support those around them—always
putting others' needs above their own. Their intentions are good
and motives sound except they maintain no margin for themselves,
leading to eventual burnout or yielding to temptation because they
neglected their needs. No wonder, then, that sooner or later these
people grow to resent what they're giving but never receiving from
themselves.

While selfless service is indeed what we see in the life of Jesus,
we must not overlook the way He also made sure His human needs
were met—for rest, for food, for community, for fellowship, for
solitude, for time with His Father. Yes, He gave His life for us sacrificially and urged His followers to die to self in order to serve others
with the love of God. But He also demonstrated an awareness of
His vulnerabilities (for example, when tempted by Satan right after
Jesus had fasted and prayed for forty days), a willingness to display
anger (at the money changers in the temple and at the Pharisees),
and a concern for His time alone with God the Father (after the
Sermon on the Mount and in Gethsemane before His arrest).

How you show up for yourself and remain present with yourself is usually shaped by the conclusions and assumptions you've
formed about who you are based on your interactions with other

people throughout your life. Beginning with birth and how your needs were handled by parents and caregivers and extending to right now with the ensemble cast of people in your life, you have formed beliefs. Unexamined and unchallenged, these beliefs remain unreliable data for who you are and how you deserve to be treated.

Others may have abandoned, betrayed, rejected, and hurt you immensely. But you have control of the messaging you take away from those experiences. You can either choose to believe lies from the enemy that you are unlovable, unlikable, unchangeable, and unredeemable. Or, you can become a student of yourself and who God says you are. You can let lazy love remain your default setting, which means looking to others to fulfill your needs and blaming them when your needs go unmet. Or, you can learn to identify your needs, meet them in healthy ways if possible, and seek God's presence, purpose, and provision in them.

DIVINE ROMANCE

Eros love allows you to be single and satisfied by the love of God before you extend its expression to others. Without being anchored by agape, sexual intimacy can become transactional and temporary, which means it becomes lust instead of relational and committed as God intends for His creation. Physical and sexual accessibility does not define intimacy. God created our sexuality to be revealed in its fullness, including its spiritual dimension. Which is why Paul reminds us that our bodies are temples of God's Spirit, not to be defined by our appetites but by our humanity infused with and anchored by agape love.

Intimacy with God precedes your intimacy with your beloved. You experience the freedom to be seen and known, accepted and loved, without shame or embarrassment. Your need for connection is not a compulsion but a divine spiritual compelling. The heartbeat of eros love is the heartbeat of God's love for us. Remembering the true meaning of eros helps you to keep showing up for yourself.

When you show up for yourself, especially if you're in a season of singleness, you celebrate the gifts that come with it. And I emphasize that singleness is a gift in and of itself... not as preparation for marriage, not as the consequence of sinful choices or past mistakes. If you don't take my word for it, consider what Paul wrote:

> I wish that all of you were as I am. But each of you has your own gift from God; one has this gift, another has that. Now to the unmarried and the widows I say: It is good for them to stay unmarried, as I do. But if they cannot control themselves, they should marry, for it is better to marry than to burn with passion. (1 Corinthians 7:7–9)

Paul regarded his singleness as a gift from God and wished others could experience it and view it this way as well. This passage occurs within the larger context of discussing marriage in a letter to believers at the early church in Corinth. We'll return to explore it more fully when we shift to marriage in the next chapter. For now, just note that Paul declares that it is good to stay unmarried—with one caveat.

He said it's better to marry than to "burn with passion." We usually assume this phrase refers to lust, but I like to consider it extending beyond sexual passion to any of the things we lust after—again, the lust of the eyes, the lust of the flesh, the pride of our human egos. With this in mind, how might marriage be better? I have some ideas and look forward to sharing them shortly.

Getting back to the gift of singleness, though, I believe many people struggle not only to show up for themselves but to show up fully in how they relate to God. They distract themselves by being on the hunt for the next potential partner or serious relationship. Rather than drawing closer to the Lord, they resist the opportunity to know Him and look for fulfillment in human form. Perpetually dating often stems from failing to recognize that relationships operate in seasons rather than time.

Waiting on God's timing, however, provides opportunities for you to heal old wounds and cultivate your capacity to love again. It gives you space to explore who God is and how you relate to Him based on past disappointments and losses. You have time to rely on Him as the loving Father who lavishes love on His precious sons and daughters. You basically learn to date the divine as He reveals just how much He cares for you and wants to be involved in your life.

If you're constantly assuming you need another person before you can have all your needs met, then I encourage you to think again. From the declaration of the poet in Psalm 23—"The LORD is my shepherd, I lack nothing" (v. 1)—to the assertion of Paul when writing to the Philippians—"And my God will meet all your needs according to the riches of his glory in Christ Jesus" (Phil. 4:19)—remember that He has always provided for you. Perhaps not the way you want, or when you want the way you want, but you are in this present moment for a reason.

You desire to love with more abandon, more joy, more peace, and more purpose and to stop relying on lazy love once and for all. If this were not the desire of your heart, you would not be reading this book as it nears its conclusion! So allow yourself to rest in the arms of the One who knows you best and loves you most. Choose to face your fears and get to know yourself, loving yourself as you long to be loved, as you often love those around you.

Whether single or married, divorced or dating, celibate or sociable, you can experience the divine heartbeat of eros. When you refuse to make your happiness and your willingness to love others contingent on your relationship status, you choose wholeness over cultural assumptions of singleness. You choose yourself over compromise. You choose God over idols and divine romance over cultural expectations. Eros love is about coming together and realizing you already know its fundamental source.

Eros love leads you away from sex objectified and segregated from the rest of the total person and back to intimacy, belonging, and fulfillment by welcoming all aspects of each individual into a shared union.

Nothing is hidden.

All is known.

Naked and unashamed.

CHAPTER 15

Marriage–Making

A good marriage is one which allows for change and growth
in the individuals and in the way they express their love.
—Pearl S. Buck

Some containers last while others can no longer retain what they were originally designed to hold. For instance, just consider the Great Wall of China, which stretches for more than thirteen thousand miles along its country's northern border. It is the largest manmade structure in the world and visible from space when looking at the earth's surface. The Great Wall is not one continuous unbroken stone barrier but rather an ongoing collection of various segments. The oldest portions date back to the seventh century BC with subsequent additions, extensions, and repairs accumulating over the centuries.[1] With roughly ten million or more tourists annually visiting this ancient wonder, it continues to intrigue us because of its sheer size and historical significance.[2]

In many ways, the Great Wall's significance lies in the fact that it has endured, an artifact bridging past centuries to the present even though its intended purpose is no longer needed or relevant. No matter how thick or high, a stone wall no longer provides adequate protection against the arsenal of sophisticated weaponry in today's world. So rather than being a defense system, the Great Wall of China has become an item on most travelers' bucket lists, an engineering curiosity and time capsule of ancient civilizations.

Sometimes I wonder if marriage in the twenty-first century resembles this ancient wonder. Something that was once essential for survival, of vital importance for keeping some things in and other things out. Something that began based on an urgent need—"it is not good for man to be alone"—but has now deteriorated into an archaic relic, still in existence and acknowledged by millions but no longer fulfilling its original purpose. Like the Great Wall, marriage used to work and helped people survive life's assaults and became an enduring legacy for each subsequent generation.

Don't get me wrong—I'm not saying that marriage is no longer relevant or important to God and His people. In fact, I am a huge fan of marriage and count mine as a blessing unique from any other with which God has graced me. But I'm also aware of the impact divorce has on individuals, families, communities, and connections. I'm aware of the way many if not most of our younger generations, millennials and those behind them, consider marriage to be a messy commitment that leaves people just as lonely and unhappy as being single. I'm aware of the legal, financial, social, and emotional ties that come with marriage, often complicating the 50 percent or so of marriages that don't work.

So even as I view marriage as something like an ancient wonder of the world, I'm also aware of marriage as a timeless sacred expression of relational eros, so sacred, in fact, that God chose to use marriage as the primary metaphor for the relationship between Christ and the church. Choosing this description emphasizes that eros and agape are closely related. While agape is the ultimate source for all forms of love, eros and its connotations of sexual and erotic pleasure have sometimes been villainized.

But eros is about so much more than sex.

Eros is about holy intimacy.

MARRIAGE IS THE METHOD

No matter how many people view marriage as archaic and outdated, it remains a sacrament that the church continues to uphold and practice. Not because of tradition or history or cultural expectations but because of how God views it. Christians have to love marriage and practice it as a sacred institution because it depicts our relationship with Jesus. There has to be fidelity and commitment, a connection expressed overtly in a formal, clear, direct way and always grounded in love.

If you view marriage critically or have lost faith in it altogether, keep in mind that its flaws are our own. A friend of mine who's a therapist likes to say, "You spot it; you got it," meaning that what we see in others, both positive and negative, often reflects those same traits and qualities within ourselves. How you consider marriage right now likely says more about where you are than where marriage is in our culture.

If you view marriage as a failed institution that's lost its meaning, it's because those practicing it have failed and allowed the significance of marriage to fade. But if you don't have the gift of singleness, then marriage is the method God uses to facilitate maximum human intimacy and connection. It is not good for you to be alone. God made us to be relational and social and connection focused. God Himself is three persons in One, modeling for us the way we can abide in Him through the Holy Spirit thanks to what was done for us through the Son, Jesus, sent because of the Father's love.

Marriage distills and refines our desire for connection into experiencing a deep and loving bond with our spouse. This relationship does not meet all of our relational and emotional needs, nor should it, but it provides the foundational elements of security, acceptance, comfort, being known, and being loved. Ideally, it facilitates the kind of secure healthy attachment we need in order to be our best self, the man or woman God created us to be.

Secure attachment, however, does not mean perfect, passive, or pacifying. Loving your spouse with selfless, sacrificial love requires attunement to God's Spirit as well as to your husband or wife. The goal is not perfect harmony, a stress-free union, or fulfilling each other's idealized expectations; the goal is experiencing divine love that liberates each of you to love your spouse in the midst of their flaws, faults, and failures. You don't need to compromise who you are and change for the other person in order to be at home in the love of your marriage.

In fact, some of the most secure, stable marriages develop between people with opposite and complementary personalities, experiences, and attitudes. I'm convinced that marriage is one of God's ways of discipling us, of teaching and sanctifying us as we become more authentic. Marriage is not the only way or the best way, but it is one way He uses to help us become more fully who He created us to be. In order to love well within marriage, you have to become more like God, the source of love.

Marriage forces us to learn to care about someone else besides ourselves.

But the threat posed by confusing sex with intimacy still persists. We tend to assume that eros love expressed by a committed husband and wife automatically and inherently reflects intimacy. This is certainly God's intention for marriage, but often our past experiences, struggles with lust, and resistance to vulnerability get in the way. Couples in counseling often seem shocked to realize that their frequency of lovemaking does not necessarily reflect the strength and depth of the intimacy they share.

Eros love brings your beloved into clear focus as your equal and complementary partner. You see and know all of them, and they see and know all of you. Shared sexuality eliminates lust when divine eros brings a man and a woman into oneness.

EROS EVOLVING

As my seasons of life have changed, my view of marriage has evolved as well. I was once under the impression that if you're not happy in the relationship with your spouse—not just annoyed or frustrated but deeply unhappy with no changes in sight—then it's probably better for each of you to be apart than together. If, after considerable attempts to communicate and resolve and alleviate, dynamics of the union cannot be changed for the better, then hard questions about your future together have to be examined.

But here's what I've realized from my own experience as well as others': Once you leave a marriage in order to be happy, you quickly discover the other things you're still unhappy about! If you're not happy internally, then you will never find it externally—not in your marriage, your career, your family, your achievements, or your possessions. Marriage never solves any emotional problems, not loneliness, insecurity, fear, or anger. Marriage simply gives you a person to reflect those problems back at you.

The other major shift in my understanding of marriage is to embrace the commitment without an escape hatch. I didn't realize it at the time, but I may have initially gone into marriage when I was much younger with an underlying belief that if the relationship didn't work out, then I had a way out. Again, I assumed if someone wasn't content and enjoying the relationship, then it was okay to end it and look elsewhere for fulfillment.

Now, however, I consider marriage a forever proposition that requires relinquishing expectations up front about how things should and will go in the relationship. The more you can be present to who your spouse actually is and not who you want them to be, the greater your opportunity for connection, collaboration, and cooperation on every level. Being present to who they are and who you are means you will sometimes—perhaps even frequently in certain seasons—experience discomfort, disappointment, frustration, and inconvenience.

Rather than trying to eliminate problems, conflicts, and disagreements, healthy marriages accept them as part of the friction inherent for sustaining the connection between the two of you. I've counseled couples who came to me because they stopped speaking to one another, allowing the silence to drive a deeper wedge into their emotional, physical, and spiritual bond. One such couple agreed to speak to me together but with the condition of not having to address their partner.

As we unraveled their wounding, the catalyst emerged as something said by the husband almost a month prior that the wife interpreted based on the story she told herself about their relationship. Both were at fault and both slowly saw the need to claim responsibility rather than retreating and resisting communication. If they had actually tried to understand one another's feelings, assumptions, and subjective narrative at the time of the offense, they could have shifted their perspective, on themselves and their spouse, much sooner.

Each of them grew up in loud, confrontational, drama-prone homes and had vowed to themselves never to repeat their parents' attitudes and behaviors in their own marriage. Without realizing it, they each withdrew and detached whenever any conflict or emotional friction developed. Becoming more aware of their own tendencies and their spouse's allowed them to realize that they had many other options for problem-solving besides to simply detach or to confront with drama. Their differences as well as shared tendencies enabled them to be more loving and attuned to one another.

And in many ways, that's the essence of healthy love—leaning into the differences, the challenges, the opposing views, the tensions and frictions. Sharing this space is where evangelism takes place in a marriage. Someone who becomes more like us will not challenge and sharpen us like the one willing to accept and love us while still disagreeing or confronting us. When we try to make our spouse bend to be more like us, or more of what we want them to be for us, we're only emphasizing our own strengths and weaknesses. If we are to grow and mature, we must be willing to experience dynamic love, the kind that causes us to change not for anyone else but for ourselves as we become more authentic to who God made us to be.

One example from my own marriage that comes to mind relates to how my wife, Shaunie, and I generally tend to view other people. I tend to have a grace for people, viewing them through a lens colored by love—the kind that is often blind. While I extend grace on the front end of a relationship, my wife tends to have an intuition to wait and extend grace down the road, after she has traveled some miles together with the other person.

My natural inclination is to accept others at face value, mostly assuming the best about them and their motives and therefore usually giving them the benefit of the doubt until I have reason to do otherwise. My wife takes a slightly different approach and often regards other people with more uncertainty and curiosity and a side of caution. She's not exactly skeptical or distrusting, but she's going to wait until her trust has been earned before assuming the best about someone.

With these different approaches, we naturally balance one another. I sometimes challenge her suspicions or cautious tendencies while she protectively helps me allow for others to show me who they are before I form impressions or conclusions. This is but one of the many ways my wife and I invest in one another's lives, stretching and shaping, nourishing and ripening the fruit of our life together. We know that loving one another just as we are makes us better people.

Together, we grow into holistic wholeness that deepens our capacity for love.

LET THE ICE MELT

As my understanding and experience of marriage has changed, I not only embrace the ways my wife is different from me, but I try to extend grace and freedom for her to be more herself. There is no one secret to creating and sustaining a healthy, vibrant marriage grounded in agape and watered by eros, but enjoying and empowering your spouse's uniqueness certainly makes a crucial positive difference. I've learned the purpose of marriage is not to try to make someone who is an individual more like you. The goal of love is to liberate your spouse from shame and doubt and insecurity and fear of rejection so that they can just be. Just experience the freedom to be themselves.

Prior to taking our vows as man and wife, Shaunie and I were in premarital counseling with Bishop T. D. Jakes. Our final session with him occurred less than twenty-four hours before we walked down the aisle on the gorgeous island of Anguilla. We were filming our conversation to include in our reality special *Destination*

"I Do," which added a little pressure to our responses because we knew countless viewers would be tuning in.

We met outside in a lovely, shaded patio area near the resort hosting our festivities. When we had been served iced tea, I noticed that Bishop Jakes placed a tumbler on the table beside him that held only ice. We proceeded with our conversation, engaging and enjoying the thoughtful questions and gleaned wisdom shared among us. Bishop Jakes generously shared the best practices and practicalities he and Mrs. Jakes had learned in their shared decades of matrimony.

Two hours quickly passed, and after a short break, we resumed our discussion of how a marriage thrives. Without missing a beat, Bishop Jakes picked up the glass that had once contained ice and drank down the cool water it had become. He smiled and said, "Sometimes when you leave something alone, it naturally becomes what it's meant to be. I didn't force this ice to melt into water that I could drink. I simply placed it in an environment so that it could naturally transform into liquid."

He proceeded to share that in his vast experience of counseling couples, both before marriage as well as afterward in the midst of struggles, he has found that the most growth takes place when each person stops being so pushy in trying to fix their spouse. Instead of insisting, either consciously or unconsciously, for their husband to be more sensitive, thoughtful, and caring, wives could let them desire and shift toward this naturally. Rather than wanting their wives to be more attentive, supportive, and physically demonstrative, husbands could relax and appreciate the woman whom they chose just as she was.

Pushing one another will not accelerate growth—only frustrate both of you. If you enjoy and accept each other, shortcomings and all, then eventually you each become more of who you're supposed to be. He will be more authentic. She will be more authentic. The love between you will demonstrate the unconditional acceptance, emotional nurturance, and divine grace that God bestows upon each of us.

This is the essence of eros.

Settling for anything less is always lazy love.

WHOLE NEW WORLD

I know firsthand, though, that lazy love can be radically transformed into eros. From my experience and that of others I know, meeting your future spouse is rarely the meet-cute of romance novels and rom-coms on the Hallmark Channel. While online meetings leading to real-life, in-person appointments still prevail for many couples, matchmaking single friends remains a pastime obsession for many BFFs, grandmas, aunties, sisters, and teammates. Shaunie and I were, in fact, introduced by a mutual friend who knew we were both single and had a hunch we might hit it off.

While she and I agreed to meet, I suspect neither of us had thought it would lead to anything more than friendship. We were both reluctant to admit that we were willing to date anyone, each of us saying that we would never marry again. When we met, both Shaunie and I were each still very affected and broken by our past relationships. We had both settled into singleness, assuming that this was the gift God had for us as we moved forward. In other words, we both stumbled into our first date with lazy love dragging us there.

And there was no instant attraction or immediate laser-gaze, eye-locking awareness of immediate love. Instead, there was a coming together of two people uncertain about what they wanted or needed in a relationship, considering all they had been through.

We were both parents of teenagers and young adult children, each comfortable in our calling, and content to rely on the Lord's timing.

Curiously enough, having no real desire or expectations for a serious relationship was incredibly freeing. We quickly abandoned lazy love and became intentional about just being present with each other when we were together. Each of us was surprised to discover the other was not exactly what we expected. Our curiosity and openness allowed us to just talk and compare stories, discuss our kids, and evaluate where we were in our lives. Because we weren't worried about impressing each other or being coy and flirty or any of the other driving forces often at play in relationships, we relaxed and just took each day, each encounter, each conversation as it was.

Knowing what I know now, I would encourage you not to start with an end in mind when you date or meet someone to whom you're attracted. You've probably met people, both women and men, who already have a vision of their future wedded bliss. They know what the theme and the venue for the wedding will be, where they'll go on their honeymoon, how many children they want, and what their home will look like. These people go on first dates and hear wedding bells in the background before they have any idea if they like one another.

Because we were in no rush and had no end in mind, we discovered more about each other than if we had declared we were seriously dating when we started. Our time together followed its own natural pace, an organic course of action determining our next steps. We weren't thinking about being together forever. We just kept showing up one day at a time. We didn't look ahead beyond the next day, if that. Even as we grew closer and began considering blending our lives together through marriage, we didn't assume or rush or second-guess what was ahead.

So often the pressures and expectations involved begin to accumulate and form an overwhelming weight. People begin worrying about whose family will visit for which holidays and who they'll see on vacations. Whose furniture to keep and whose to lose, which toaster and microwave, on and on and on. Layers add up and suffocate the spontaneity and limit the love growing between you.

Once you're married, continue to take your relationship one day at a time. Don't race into mythic milestones. When you get married, everything doesn't change because your name or address does. Marriage bridges two histories, two continents of life lived, two people coming together who view the world in totally different ways. The magic of marriage is not about converting or hijacking the other to your world but about creating a new and different world of your own together.

You converge to build a whole new world you can both live in together.

A world that is whole because you are both required.

One that is new and has never existed before you two came together.

RIGHT IN FRONT OF YOU

Finally, let me say that if you desperately want to experience eros love, then stop looking, perhaps even stop dating. The harder you work to make it happen, the more elusive eros love often becomes. With this kind of love, I suspect the old adage is true: When the student is ready, the teacher will appear. Only in this case, when the student is ready, they will meet another student and become each other's teacher.

Too many people can't find an eros relationship because they're working so hard to make it happen. I'm reminded of a post I saw on

Instagram or TikTok recently in which this teenage son pranked his dad just as the dad was about to leave for work. The son texted: "U left your phone in the house. Want it?" Sixty seconds later the dad rushed back in the door and looked at the son, who was working hard to keep a poker face. "Well, where is it? You said you saw my phone." By then the son had burst out laughing because his dad had fallen for it even while standing there with his phone in his hand.

Looking for eros love is often like that. We think we're missing something essential, but it's already right in front of us, already part of our lives. It may not look like what we expect or be whom we envision. It may have little to do with sex appeal or physical attraction and everything to do with soul chemistry and heart attunement. Like the glasses perched on your head as you frantically look for them, you finally pause and realize you already have what you need.

Eros love does not always lead to marriage, but marriage should always be kindled by eros love. Marriage relies on the capacity to love in all four of these biblical areas we've explored—*agape*, *phileo*, *storge*, and *eros*. Committing to love another person for the rest of your lives requires a hybrid blend of gratitude, grace, and gravity to be anchored to God together in the present. The more you love God and experience His love, the greater your capacity to love your spouse—and others—becomes.

Love Is Proactive

This is my command: Love one another the way I loved you.
This is the very best way to love.

—John 15:12–13 MSG

No matter what threats you encounter in your relationships, lazy love will not win. Because once you have experienced divine love, it changes everything. The way you love is no longer reactive but proactive! You can first love others because God has first loved you.

Lazy love may have become your default setting, but it no longer determines who you are and how you love yourself, God, and others. With agape as your foundation, you discover and explore both giving and receiving love in all its forms. You realize that with God as its source, true love is never lazy but always active, resilient, dynamic, compassionate, and joyful. As you become more mindful of wanting love, refusing to settle for less, and experiencing more active love, the old lazy default tendencies of your past will recede and fade. Because the sense of contentment and satisfaction produced by true love, with your heart full and your soul at peace, becomes the essence of who you are.

You no longer need to settle because your heart has been awakened.

Relationships were never intended to be "complicated."

You were made to experience loving relationships in ways that inspire, stimulate, challenge, accept, comfort, and motivate you. To be known without any defenses or pretenses, any posturing or positioning. To be aware of what you truly deserve rather than what you've been willing to settle for.

Now that you are aware of the threats posed by settling for lazy love, you can not only know better but relate differently. You can rely on receiving and experiencing God's love to fill you and fuel you. You can embrace knowing that you are made for deep, trustworthy, meaningful connections with other men and women. You can bask in the freedom to love with abandon, to give love without expecting anything in return, to forgive—yourself and others—when you fall short of love, and to enjoy the fruits of sacred relationships, including trust, honesty, open communication, security, attunement, affection, and intimacy.

You can overcome the weeds of lazy love in the garden of your heart.

As we conclude our time together within these pages, I would like to share my hope and prayer for you through a paraphrase of Paul's familiar description of love from 1 Corinthians 13:[1]

> May your love wait when there's no reason to hope and when you feel impatient.
>
> May your love refuse to brag or trash-talk, cast shade or get jealous.
>
> May your love forget to hold grudges, remember to release anger, and lose sight of self-interests.

Conclusion

May your love celebrate what is true and authentic, not
   what is false and deceptive.
May your love forever guard, reach, climb, forgive, endure,
   and thrive.
May your love never fail.

ACKNOWLEDGMENTS

To my dear mother, you sent me the most beautiful text message on Thursday, February 29th at 7:50 p.m. You said, "Hey son! I want you to know that you are the anchor of my life." What you don't know is that tears streamed down my face because I didn't know that we had switched places. Thank you for encouraging me in all of my pursuits and inspiring me to follow my dreams. I hope this book shows you that you didn't waste your time by going through the pain of birthing me. I love you forever!

NOTES

CHAPTER 1

1 Shelley E. Kohan, "Valentine's Day Spending Is Expected to Hit $26 Billion, One of the Highest on Record," February 3, 2023, https://www.forbes.com/sites /shelleykohan/2023/02/03/cupid-is-not-fretting-over-higher-prices-for -valentines-day/?sh=35386aab109f.

2 Lisa Bitel, "The Real St. Valentine Was No Patron Saint of Love," February 13, 2018, The Conversation, https://theconversation.com/the-real-st-valentine-was-no-patron -of-love-90518?gclid=Cj0KCQiAxbefBhDfARIsAL4XLRoTTwh OYnTpcxsrkV3SzsCJG6yG_6Jy7CUJjgPPyCgw6Ucme-I_vy8aAnnAEAL w_wcB.

CHAPTER 2

1 History.com editors, "Alexander the Great," updated September 22, 2023, https: //www.history.com/topics/ancient-greece/alexander-the-great.

2 History.com editors, "Alexander the Great."

3 Helen Fisher, quoted in Katherine Wu, "Love, Actually: The Science Behind Lust, Attraction, and Companionship," February 14, 2017, SITNBoston (blog), https://sitn.hms.harvard.edu/flash/2017/love-actually-science-behind-lust -attraction-companionship/.

4 Fisher, quoted in Wu, "Love, Actually."

5 Fisher, quoted in Wu, "Love, Actually."

6 Fisher, quoted in Wu, "Love, Actually."

CHAPTER 3

1 Attachment Project, https://www.attachmentproject.com/attachment-theory/.

2 Attachment Project.

CHAPTER 5

1 C. S. Lewis, The Four Loves (San Francisco: HarperOne, 2017), 34.

CHAPTER 6

1 Odelya Gertel Kraybill, "Attunement and Love in Psychotherapy," Psychology Today, January 31, 2021, https://www.psychologytoday.com/us/blog/expressive -trauma-integration/202101/attunement-and-love-in-psychotherapy.

CHAPTER 7

1 Julie Beck, "What It's Like to Carry On a Friendship with a Friend Who Can't Rememer It," Atlantic, January, 22, 2021, https://www.theatlantic.com/family /archive/2021/01/friends-who-high-five-every-week/617775/.

2   Katherine Dillinger, "Surgeon General Lays Out Framework to Tackle Loneliness and 'Mend the Social Fabric of Our Nation,'" CNNhealth, May 2, 2023, https://www.cnn.com/2023/05/02/health/murthy-loneliness-isolation/index.html.

3   Dillinger, "Surgeon General Lays Out Framework."

CHAPTER 8

1   "Blest Be the Tie That Binds," words by John Fawcett, 1782; music by Johann G. Nägeli; arr. by Lowell Mason, 1845.

CHAPTER 11

1   Scott Dutfield and Tanya Lewis, "Human Heart: Anatomy, Function & Facts," updated July 27, 2022, Live Science, https://www.livescience.com/34655-human-heart.html.

2   "Who Was Dr. Daniel Hale Williams?," Jackson State University, https://www.jsums.edu/gtec/dr-daniel-hale-williams/.

3   Marilyn Yalom, "How Did the Human Heart Become Associated with Love?," ideas.ted.com, February 12, 2019, https://ideas.ted.com/how-did-the-human-heart-become-associated-with-love-and-how-did-it-turn-into-the-shape-we-know-today/.

4   *Easton's Bible Dictionary*, s.v. "heart," https://www.biblestudytools.com/dictionary/heart/.

5   Adolphe Adam, Christmas hymn, "O Holy Night" (n.p.: W. F. Sudds, 1883), notated music, https://www.loc.gov/item/2023849567/

CHAPTER 13

1   C. S. Lewis, *Mere Christianity* (San Francisco: HarperOne, 2023), 63.

CHAPTER 15

1   "China's Great Wall Is 'Longer Than Previously Thought,'" BBC News, June 6, 2012, https://www.bbc.com/news/world-asia-china-18337039.

2   Gaurav Gupta, "Great Wall of China: The Complete Travel Guide for First-Time Visitors in 2024," Triangle Travel, https://traveltriangle.com/blog/great-wall-of-china/#:~:text=The%20Great%20Wall%20of%20China,of%20the%20world%20every%20year.

CONCLUSION

1   "Love is patient, love is kind. It does not envy, it does not boast, it is not proud. It does not dishonor others, it is not self-seeking, it is not easily angered, it keeps no record of wrongs. Love does not delight in evil but rejoices with the truth. It always protects, always trusts, always hopes, always perseveres. Love never fails" (1 Cor. 13:4–8).

ABOUT THE AUTHOR

Bestselling author and treasured spiritual leader **Keion D. Henderson** is founder, CEO, and senior pastor of the Lighthouse Church and Ministries, one of America's fastest-growing churches, headquartered in Houston, Texas. His ministries and initiatives are fueling the explosive growth and far-reaching impact of the Lighthouse Church, whose congregation continues to blossom with more than 15,000 dedicated members and over 800,000 unique weekly viewers worldwide across all social media platforms. With more than twenty-six years in active ministry, Pastor Henderson is known for educating, nurturing, and equipping his congregants with life-changing lessons to navigate their faith with sound values and biblical principles via his accelerator for entrepreneurship. Through the weight of his words, impeccable judgment, and sophisticated understanding of the forces shaping the world, Pastor Henderson delivers the word of God with rapid-fire precision among a new generation of believers as he continues to keep faith relevant in today's culture. Pastor Henderson is a passionate humanitarian yielding a steadfast commitment who cares deeply about the plight of the people and gives back to the global communities he serves through his nonprofit Take Action Now. Recognized by the John Maxwell Institute as one of the top 250 leaders in the nation, Pastor Keion Henderson, born in Gary, Indiana, is a devoted father to his beautiful daughter, Katelyn, and a devoted husband to his forever wife, Shaunie Henderson.